OHIO'S TROJAN HORSE

A Warning
To
Christian Schools Everywhere

by
Alan N. Grover, B.A., M.A.
Executive Director, Christian Schools of Ohio

BOB JONES UNIVERSITY PRESS, INC.
GREENVILLE, SOUTH CAROLINA 29614

Ohio's Trojan Horse

ISBN 0-89084-061-X

Printed in the United States of America.

**Dedicated
To**

The Rev. Levi W. Whisner
and his co-defendants,
who recognized the dangers
of Ohio's Trojan Horse
and "withstood in the
evil day" so that their children
and children throughout our land
might have the freedom to receive
a Christian education.

Table Of Contents

Foreword

Any honest reader, whether saint or sinner, that will peruse the pages of *Ohio's Trojan Horse* without prejudice will, I believe, come to agree with the Ohio Supreme Court's decision in *Ohio v. Whisner.* The Court said that to follow these state-imposed standards would remove all differences from public education and parochial, or church-related education.

I believe that an honest evaluation of many church-related schools will show this to be the truth. Those who have given to Caesar that which belongs to God are traitors to the Christian Faith, whether knowingly or ignorantly.

Fundamentalists have long been attacked, being accused of unscholarly statements, biased reporting and narrow-minded thinking. In this book none of these accusations will hold up. Here is a book into which much work, research, and prayer have gone.

May God use it in our battle of Christian education versus Secular Humanism.

Dr. Roy Thompson
Pastor, Cleveland Baptist Church
President, Christian Schools of Ohio

Preface

On December 12, 1975, the trustees and legal counsel for Christian Schools of Ohio — more often known as CSO — met in the conference room of the Governor's office with Dr. Martin Essex, Ohio's Superintendent of Public Instruction, a cadre of members of the State Board of Education, and several representatives of the State Department of Education. The meeting had been arranged by Governor Rhodes four days after an assembly of some 10,000 Bible-believing Christians rallied on the Statehouse lawn in protest of the lawsuit that threatened to take children away from their parents because the parents had sent their children to a church-operated Christian school not licensed ("chartered") by the state.

The meeting was called by the Governor so that the Christian schools and the state's educational bureaucrats could air their respective views. Speaking for Christian Schools of Ohio was the Rev. Dr. Roy Thompson, president of Christian Schools of Ohio. While the local television cameras whirred Dr. Thompson read a brief statement in which he expressed the position of CSO. Concerning the Ohio Minimum Standards, which had precipitated the prosecutions in Ohio, Dr. Thompson declared that these Minimum Standards, as they are now constituted and enforced, were "unliveable" for Christian schools. It was that statement which launched the effort resulting in this present study. Dr. Thompson, CSO attorney David C. Gibbs, the CSO trustees, and other members of CSO had recognized the insidious danger of the Ohio Minimum Standards. Extensive efforts by these courageous Christian leaders had alerted many to the danger, but there were — and are — still many people who did not understand the issues involved in the *Canal Winchester* case.

Even during the tempest of the *Canal Winchester* matter, another Christian school case in Ohio was pending before the Ohio Supreme Court. This was the case of the Rev. Levi W. Whisner and his twelve co-defendants, who had been convicted as criminals for sending their children to a Christian school not licensed by the State of Ohio. They had argued that such licensure of their church-operated school violated their religious convictions, but had lost the first two rounds of their struggle for religious liberty. The case was heard before the Ohio Supreme Court on March 16, 1976, and the ruling was delivered by the Court on July 28, 1976. This landmark decision, known as the *Whisner* decision, has done much to alert Christians to the vital and substantive issues raised by the Christian school lawsuits in Ohio. The *Whisner* ruling vindicated the brave stand of Pastor Whisner and his co-defendants as it simultaneously corroborated the position of CSO and Dr. Thompson.

This writer was present in the Governor's conference room on December 12, 1975 as the soon-to-be-installed Executive Director of Christian Schools of Ohio. A logically reasoned defense, an "apologetic" of the CSO position, inspired by Dr. Thompson's statement, became one of the first concerns of the new director. The positional statement began as a "fact sheet," but quickly grew to a paper. The first paper was completed by the end of January, 1976, and filled about twenty typewritten pages. Further research and rewriting, occasioned by the advice of CSO attorney David C. Gibbs, postponed publication of the paper so that the Whisner decision intervened. The favorable ruling of the Court required yet another rewriting, and the paper grew into a small book. While we might wish that this book had been published long ago, we remember the promise of Romans 8:28, and we recognize that the delays encountered were of the Lord.

This study, then, is sent forth with the prayer that the Lord will use it to clarify the understanding and fortify the scriptural stand of Bible-believing Christians both in Ohio and in other states as well. The Christian school movement has been mightily used of God, and it may continue to be so — if it is not brought under the control of the state. May the Lord help us to avoid that end.

The author wishes to express sincere appreciation to the people whose help made this study possible. Pastor Levi Whisner and the good people involved in the Bradford Christian school case placed conviction above convenience, and the Lord blessed their courageous and sometimes lonely stand. Constitutional lawyer William B. Ball, of Harrisburg, Pennsylvania, well known for his defense of religious liberty, argued the case for the defense in the *Whisner* trial. Dr. Roy Thompson has sacrificed personal ease and displayed Christian boldness in his leadership of CSO. Attorney David C. Gibbs, along with his associates (Charles Craze, Brian Thompson, Fred P. Benco, and Michael Manuszak) have provided invaluable assistance, guidance, and instruction in legal matters. The firm of Gibbs, Craze, and Thompson also prepared an excellent brief of *amici curiae* for over a hundred Ohio ministers who supported Rev. Whisner and his co-defendants before the Ohio Supreme Court.

The Rev. Rousas J. Rushdoony, of Vallecito, California, has graciously written the introduction to this study. Dr. Rushdoony's instruction, both in his written works and in person, has been extremely helpful. The foresight and depth of his observations serve all Christians in the ongoing struggle to defend our faith and our children. Dr. Rushdoony's kind encouragement in this work is also deeply appreciated.

The author would like to thank Mr. Raymond H. Davis, the Sales Manager of Arrow Office Equipment, Inc., Cleveland, Ohio, for assistance that made possible the production of the manuscript.

The author would also like to thank Dr. Jack R. Riggs and the Rev. James M. Grier, both professors at the Cedarville College, Cedarville, Ohio, for valuable assistance in the research of Secular Humanism and educational philosophy. The suggestions of the Rev. Joseph Lewis, a CSO trustee and pastor of the Trinity Baptist Temple, Middletown, Ohio, are thankfully remembered. Rev. Lewis is also the plaintiff in a taxpayer suit contesting the promulgation of Secular Humanism in the public schools of his local district. His insights have been most helpful.

Appreciation is expressed to Mr. Elmer Rumminger and Mr. George Collins of the Bob Jones University Press, Inc., for their many helpful suggestions, and to the BJU Press for publication of this work. The Rev. John E. Ashbrook, Bible Community Church, Mentor, Ohio, read much of the manuscript and offered valuable suggestions. The author grew up under the teaching ministry of Rev. Ashbrook, then served as his associate pastor for over two and a half years. Pastor Ashbrook's encouragement is deeply appreciated.

The Rev. Frank R. Hamblen, Calvary Bible Church, Lima, Ohio, is a trustee of CSO and father-in-law of the author. He was the author's most determined encourager in the lengthy job of research and revision of this manuscript. Pastor Hamblen also read the pre-publication manuscript and offered helpful suggestions. These efforts are gratefully remembered. Finally, the support and assistance of the author's wife are deeply appreciated.

The issues addressed in this study are as real as the cold clang of steel on steel within a prison. The threats of imprisonment which face godly Christian people in the free exercise of their religious convictions today are likewise startlingly real. The author's prayer is that God may use this work as a warning, and that the lessons learned under fire in Ohio may serve as valuable instruction for Christians in other states as well.

Rev. Alan N. Grover
Executive Director
Christian Schools of Ohio

6929 W. 130th St. — Suite 600
Cleveland, Ohio 44130
phone: (216) 845-6806

Introduction

The battle for the future of both Christianity and the United States is now underway, and the battleground is the Christian school. The Ohio struggle therefore is of central importance: it is the first battle in a war which will be the most important aspect of our history for the next decade at least.

Control of children and their education is control of the future. Humanists have always understood this. Horace Mann, James G. Carter, and their many associates (including Senator Charles Sumner), were all Unitarians; they hated the Puritan faith of their forefathers with a passion. Their purpose in promoting state control of education was twofold. *First,* they rightfully understood that the only way to destroy Biblical faith was to control the schools and, little by little, remove Christianity and introduce Humanism. *Second,* they were Centralists or statists, men who believed that salvation comes by works of statist legislation or law.

Horace Mann believed that, after a century of public schools, crime and other problems would disappear from America, and prisons would be only a relic of our foolish, erroneous, and evangelical past. A century and half has almost passed, and, instead of Horace Mann's Millennium, we have all the social and moral breakdown which humanistic education has promoted. The statist educators have indeed controlled America's future by controlling its schools; they have made the curriculum of those schools more and more openly humanistic and anti-Christian. The results are very much with us.

To surrender our children to anti-Christian, humanistic schools is to deny Christ. It is a greater evil than putting our children into modernist Sunday Schools and churches. A church, after all, "commands" only two or three hours of a child's time a week, whereas the state schools literally command our children five full days a week, if we submit them to this modern Moloch.

Remember, Moloch means *king*. Moloch worship was state worship. It meant that the state had life and death power over its citizens and could command their children for life or death. Moloch worship is forbidden in Scripture. What Pastor Levi Whisner, Attorneys William Ball and David C. Gibbs, Jr., and others in Ohio have done is to resist Moloch worship.

Control of children is control of the future, and control over us, our children, and the future belongs only to our Lord Jesus Christ. We cannot surrender our children to the enemy without denying our Lord.

The enemy cannot win if a large number of children are brought up in the nurture and admonition of their Lord. A God-fearing nucleus of resistance to Humanism will then exist. Hence the great effort to turn Christian schools into agencies of Humanism.

In *A Common Faith,* John Dewey in 1934 spelled out the religion of Humanism. Its goal is democracy. This means that there can be no differences nor distinctions, such as between heaven and hell, good and evil, right and wrong, or the saved and the lost. All such distinctions perpetuate a spirit of aristocracy. Evangelical Christianity and democracy, Dewey held, are incompatible; Biblical religion must make way for Humanism.

The battle for the Christian schools is thus the battle for the faith. We are in the most important and crucial war of religion in all history, the struggle between Christianity and Humanism. Where do you stand in this battle? It is a war unto death, and the goal of the enemy is the obliteration of our faith. If this battle is nothing to you, the Lord may soon declare that you are nothing to Him.

Rev. Rousas John Rushdoony
Vallecito, California 95251

Explanatory Note

Throughout this study we have sought to follow a consistent format in the capitalization of "Minimum Standards." In our research we have found no consistent usage as to capitalization. Sometimes we find "minimum standards," sometimes "Minimum Standards," and sometimes we find the title of the document both capitalized and italicized.

We regard the second usage as the proper one, simply because the Ohio elementary minimum standards comprise an entire volume. In order to simplify this study, however, we have adopted the following rule of thumb: when discussing the *volume* of standards we have used "Minimum Standards," and when discussing *individual* standards we have written "minimum standards." This formula, of course, is not followed either in the statutory law or the court opinions which we have cited. The legal cites generally use only the lower case letters.

CSO has long contended that the Ohio Minimum Standards are not minimum at all, for they are so extensive and prescriptive that "minimum" is decidedly a misnomer. Neither are these requirements "maximum standards," for they do not lead to an education of maximum quality. We are certain that we could devise a more appropriate title than "minimum standards," but since the State educationists would quite likely decide against its use, we will not invest the effort.

We note with interest that when the Ohio Supreme Court mentions the "minimum standards" in the Whisner opinion, they regularly place the name within a set of quotation marks. Because that Court has recognized that the standards are *not* truly minimum, we suggest that the Court, like CSO, may be indicating in this manner their discomfort in using the term "minimum" as applied to these standards.

We also note that this study examines the *Minimum Standards for Ohio Elementary Schools, Revised 1970.* It does not specifically treat the "minimum standards" for either junior high or high schools. The reader will discover, however, that some of the issues raised as to the elementary standards are also applicable to the secondary standards as well.

The reader will also notice differences of capitalization for the term "Secular Humanism." The explanation for these differences will be found within this study, in chapter 5, on page 41 and will not, therefore, be recounted here.

1

Preliminary Considerations

When Christian Schools of Ohio (CSO) states that the Ohio Minimum Standards, as they are presently constituted and enforced, are "unliveable for Christian schools," some people wonder if our schools are shirking the responsibility of providing their students with a quality education. This is a complete misunderstanding of the problem. This study is sent out to clarify the issues of the problem, and to spell out our objections to the Ohio Minimum Standards and their inherent state control of church-operated schools.

This study deals with two areas of concern: local and national. It examines, first, the specific complaints raised by Bible-believing, Fundamentalist Christians in the State of Ohio. The legal prosecutions endured by Christian schools in Ohio are well known to Christians and Christian educators nationwide, and many fellow Christians in other states have expressed the desire to better understand the issues involved in the Ohio cases.

Second, this study will also examine certain general issues of vital concern to Christians and Christian educators everywhere. Although these issues are integral to the Ohio struggle, they havc been and are being duplicated in many other states. The magnitude and implications of these issues require a familiarity and understanding by all Bible-believing Christians. Christian pastors and other Christian educators, and especially Christian parents, must formulate systematic positional statements that are consistent with the teaching of God's Word on these subjects. This study is a systematic positional statement for the Christian Schools of Ohio (CSO), but we believe our brethren in other states — as well as other Christian schools in our own state — will profit by reading and understanding the concomitant issues in the Ohio maelstrom.

Three issues that require national attention and inspection are (1) the matter of Secular Humanism, which many recognize as the regnant philosophy in American education today, (2) the question of responsibility for the education and upbringing of children (is the primary responsibility statist or parental?), and (3) the state control of church-operated Christian schools which is inherent in *any* state licensure or chartering of Christian schools. These are the issues which have fomented the Ohio prosecutions, and these the issues which imbue the Ohio cases with both instruction and warning for all Christians who live, teach, and preach within our constitutional republic.

There exist some similarities between the Ohio Minimum Standards and the Trojan Horse of Homer's epic poem, the *Iliad.* Our readers probably remember the story. The Greeks had laid seige to the fortified city of Troy for ten years, but neither side could defeat the other. Finally, however, the stratagem of the Trojan Horse was conceived by the Greek hero, Ulysses. A huge wooden horse was built and rolled before the gates of Troy. The Trojans were told that it was a gift for the goddess Athena, and they watched as the Greek fleet sailed away from Troy.

To bring the lofty horse into the city was a great temptation to the Trojans. A priest of the city, Laocoön, cautioned his countrymen against the wiles of the Greeks and almost succeeded in effecting the destruction of the horse outside the walls of Troy.

At the last minute a Greek prisoner, who had been planted in Troy, convinced the Trojans to disregard the warning and take the horse into their city. They opened wide their gates, and amid great joy and celebration they rolled the horse into Troy.

During the celebration that night, the Greek prisoner opened a door on the side of the horse, and out came the Greek soldiers who were waiting inside. The Greeks inside the city quickly flung open the gates, thus permitting their comrades (who had since returned) to storm the city. The Trojans were killed and their city was burned.

The Trojans were defeated for one essential reason: they brought the Trojan Horse into their fortress without finding out what was inside.

The Minimum Standards are similar to the Trojan Horse. The very name sounds harmless. The volume containing the standards is externally attractive. We are told that following the Minimum Standards is the path to quality schools, and everyone is for quality schools. But what is inside? Is the material on the inside of such a nature as to allow a church-operated school, and more particularly, a Christian school, to embrace this document without sustaining irreparable damages?

CSO says no. And to support our answer we must take our readers into the courtroom with those Christians from Ohio who have defended this position in the courts of our state. We maintain that Christian schools are unable to comply with the requirements of the Minimum Standards without destroying thereby their purpose for existence. We view this document as an intrusion by the state into the religious free exercise of Ohio's citizenry. With this position in mind, let us turn our attention to the origin of our innocently-labeled Trojan Horse, in order that we may understand its purpose more fully.

THE ORIGIN OF THE MINIMUM STANDARDS

In the mid-fifties the Ohio General Assembly passed into law the statutes which established the present form of the State Board of Education. The State Board was empowered by section 3301.07 of the Ohio Revised Code to "formulate and prescribe minimum standards to be applied to all elementary and high schools in this state. . . ." Pursuant to this authority the first minimum standards were developed and became effective on April 15, 1957.

The 1957 standards were developed "through a series of conferences with school superintendents, principals, supervisors, teachers, and representatives of private and parochial schools in Ohio."[1] One purpose of the standards was to set the minimum limits for the legal definition of a school. This thought was expressed as follows:

> It is the desire of the State Board of Education to record that these standards are minimum only; that they are not optimum standards. It is the intention of the board to hereby adopt standards below which no elementary

> school may fall. An institution which does not meet these standards shall not be considered to be a school within the meaning of Chapter 3321 of the Revised Code, the Compulsory Attendance Law.[2]

This explanation in the original standards portended the course of litigation which would be applied, under a new set of standards, almost two decades later, against a number of our Christian schools.

Toward the end of the sixties the State Board of Education apparently decided that a revision of the standards was necessary. Again committees met, proposals were considered, and the minimum standards were revised. The revised compilation of standards contained, as did the original, an "Interpretative and Explanatory" section, which had also been revised and expanded. This new set of standards, which went into effect in July, 1970, is the present set of "minimum standards" about which this study is written. Having briefly reviewed the origin of the current Minimum Standards, let us now consider the purpose for which they were created.

THE PURPOSE OF THE MINIMUM STANDARDS

As we have seen, section 3301.07 of the Ohio Revised Code authorized the State Board of Education to formulate and prescribe minimum standards. This section also gave the purpose for the standards:

> [The State Board of Education] shall formulate and prescribe minimum standards to be applied to all elementary and high schools in this state *for the purpose of requiring a general education of high quality.* [Emphasis added]

The stated purpose of the Minimum Standards is to require a high-quality education. If the Standards that were later formulated to satisfy this purpose could be shown to be arbitrary, educationally indefensible, suffocating to educational and religious liberty, unconstitutional, and religiously offensive, we would have to conclude that they had not fulfilled their intended purpose.

The above-quoted statute provides certain limitations of power for the Minimum Standards as applied to nonpublic schools. Since our Christian, non-tax supported schools are nonpublic schools, this part of the statute is very important to us. The law, then, requires that:

> In the formulation and administration of such standards for nonpublic schools, *the board shall also consider the particular needs, methods and objectives of said*

schools, provided they do not conflict with the provision of a general education of a high quality and provided that regular procedures shall be followed for promotion from grade to grade of pupils who have met the educational requirements prescribed. [Emphasis added]

CSO believes that the "particular needs, methods, and objectives" of our Christian schools have been ignored rather than considered, both in the formulation, and especially in the administration of these standards. Furthermore, the question of whether a quality education is being provided by our schools has not even been asked. The May, 1974, case *Ohio* v. *Whisner* is a case in point. The Whisner case has been widely reported elsewhere and the background of the case needs only to be briefly mentioned here. Those who are unfamiliar with the case but desire more information may contact the office of Christian Schools of Ohio.

Thirteen parents whose children were attending the Tabernacle Christian School, in Bradford, Ohio, were criminally indicted and convicted for "failure to send children to school," or truancy. These charges were brought because the Christian school involved did not meet all of the Minimum Standards under consideration herein, and because the school was not a "chartered" or state-approved school. We must also note that the school was not chartered or approved because the governing body of the school *did not want state approval.* The defendants argued that the Minimum Standards violated their religious convictions and unduly burdened the free exercise of their religion.

The case was heard in the Common Pleas Court of Darke County, Ohio, in May of 1974. Later that year a verdict of guilty was pronounced upon the parents. The matter was appealed to the Court of Appeals for Darke County, and on June 13, 1975, that Court affirmed the convictions. Once again the defendants appealed their case, this time to the Ohio Supreme Court. The oral arguments were heard before the Court on March 16, 1976, and on July 28, 1976, the decision was rendered. The Supreme Court of Ohio reversed the judgment of the lower courts, and the defendants were discharged. The reasons for this reversal will be seen as our objections to the Minimum Standards are considered and explained.

After the original trial began, the parents indicted in the *Whisner* case quickly discovered that the "needs, methods, and objectives" of their school were of absolutely no concern to the prosecutor representing the state of Ohio. The question of "an education of high quality" was likewise summarily dismissed by the state prosecutor as being "irrelevant and immaterial."[3]

This attitude of the state was seen as the defense attorney, William B. Ball, prepared to enter into evidence the Stanford Achievement Test scores of the children in the Tabernacle Christian School. These scores revealed that ninety percent of the children tested in Pastor Whisner's school had made between one and two year's academic progress in eight months' time.[4] While reporting these scores Attorney Ball was interrupted with this objection by the prosecutor:

> Your Honor, at this time I would renew my objection which has been continuing on any testimony on religion, or *upon the school* at the Tabernacle Christian School, being irrelevant and immaterial. [emphasis added][5]

The testimony being given "upon the school," or about the school, was, of course, the test results which showed the excellent academic progress that had been made by the school's students in its very first year of operation.

Statutory Purpose Ignored

The above statement from the Whisner trial reveals the heart of the conflict in Ohio between the educational bureaucracy and the Christian schools of the state. Our schools have been prosecuted, not on the question "Do they provide an education of high quality?" but on the question "Do they conform to the bureaucratically prescribed plan of education?" Not quality but conformity has been the criterion for judgment. The statutory purpose for the Minimum Standards — quality — is shunted aside in deference to state control.

Lest we suppose that this attitude was limited to the state's prosecutor, a brief of *amicus curiae* was filed against the cause of Pastor Whisner and his co-defendants as their case was pending before the Ohio Supreme Court. This brief was filed by Dr. Martin W. Essex, the Superintendent of Public Instruction for the State of Ohio. In this brief the man at the helm of the state educational bureaucracy argued that even if the defendants proved that their religious convictions had been violated by the Minimum Standards, the state must be given authority to overrule those convictions. Here are the words of the *amicus* brief:

> If defendants have presented evidence sufficient to support a claim of religious infringement by the State through its Minimum Standards, must the religious freedom necessarily prevail? Clearly not. . . .[6]
>
> Even if defendants were to have stated a claim for relief

> under the Free Exercise Clause, the State's interests in providing for a compulsory minimum standard of education clearly outweighs whatever minor infringement on defendants' religious practices may result.[7]

"Minor infringement?" We shall consider that assessment in the remainder of this paper. But the thrust of these statements is clear, and it has come from the "chief administrative officer"[8] of the State Department of Education. State control and the enforcement of the State's Minimum Standards seem to outweigh all other concerns, including religious convictions and the demonstration of solid academic progress on the part of those who do not feel free to comply with the State's Standards. And all this in the face of an explicit statutory order to take into consideration the "particular needs, methods, and objectives"[9] of the nonpublic schools.

SUMMARY

We have reviewed the origin and purpose of the Minimum Standards, and have learned that they were intended to require an education of high quality for students in this state. We have also seen that the Standards have been considered as more important than religious convictions and solid academic progress in a church-operated nonpublic school. Furthermore, we have seen how the State can use the Minimum Standards to impose State control over the operation of a church-related school. Having considered this introduction to Ohio's Trojan Horse, we are now ready to take a closer look at what is on the inside.

[1]Ohio, State Board of Education, *Elementary School Standards*, April 15, 1957 (Columbus, Ohio: F. J. Heer Printing Company, 1960), p. 6.

[2]Ibid, p. 9.

[3]Transcript of Testimony, p. 282, *Ohio* v. *Whisner*, 47 Ohio St. 2d 181 (1976).

[4]Ibid, p. 288.

[5]Ibid, p. 282.

[6]Brief of *amicus curiae* for the Superintendent of Public Instruction, *Ohio* v. *Whisner*, 47 Ohio St. 2d 181 (1976), p. 12.

[7]Ibid, p. 20.

[8]Ohio Revised Code, Sec. 3301.13.

[9]Ohio Revised Code, Sec. 3301.07 D.

2

According to the Experts

> The "minimum standards" under attack herein effectively repose power in the state Department of Education to control the essential elements of non-public education in this state. *The expert testimony received in this regard unequivocably demonstrates the absolute suffocation of independent thought and educational policy, and the effective retardation of religious philosophy engendered by application of these "minimum standards"* to non-public educational institutions. [Emphasis added]

"The expert testimony," said the Ohio Supreme Court, "unequivocably demonstrates the absolute suffocation. . ." that comes by application of the Minimum Standards to nonpublic schools. The Court was referring to the testimony of Mr. Ralph O'Neal West and Professor Donald A. Erickson, both of whom testified concerning the Minimum Standards during the Whisner trial. Both of these educational experts specialize in the area of nonpublic education.

The Supreme Court recognized, after hearing these men testify, that the realm of educational philosophy and methodology is quite amenable to divergence of opinion. If eminently qualified experts can so easily disagree, from whence does the state assume the right to restrict education to the form which it, the state, deems best?

The testimony presented below was given in the original Whisner trial, under oath, by experts in the field of education. These statements have been selected from the transcript of testimony of that trial, and are a matter of public record. There is more in the transcript for anyone desiring to read it, but we believe that this sample will enable our readers to see at least two major objections against the Minimum Standards.

First, the Minimum Standards are faulty in their composition. They are unclear, self-contradictory, confusing, and unreasonably arbitrary. Second, the Minimum Standards exceed the bounds of compelling state interest and are thereby unconstitutional in their prescription. They demand more from a nonpublic school than the state has the right to demand. They demand compliance with one narrow plan of education without any proof that the state plan is best, or even that it is good.

While we examine the testimony, watching for these two points to be covered, it will be helpful to remember that these statements were made orally. Oral speech, when reduced to writing, often seems somewhat disjointed. Those speaking had no opportunity to edit, rewrite, or smooth out their statements, and these statements were made under the pressure of the witness stand. The meaning of the testimony, nevertheless, was abundantly clear.

TESTIMONY OF RALPH O'NEAL WEST

Mr. Ralph West, of Wellesley, Massachusetts, is the Director of Evaluation for the Commission on Independent Secondary Schools of the New England Association of Schools and Colleges. A graduate of the Harvard College, the Harvard Graduate College, and the Harvard Graduate School of Education, he has taught extensively and served as an administrator in numerous private schools. Mr. West has spent virtually all of his time with the New England Association of Schools and Colleges working on problems of evaluation for nonpublic schools.[2] The following statements are his answers to questions concerning the *Minimum Standards for Ohio Elementary Schools, Revised 1970*.

Mr. West was asked by defense attorney William Ball to give his general observations concerning the Minimum Standards.

> West. First of all, I would like to say that my examination of these standards would indicate that there is an apparent failure in the document to spell out clearly the procedures for a school seeking approval.[3]

Secondly, I find the wording confusing in places and vague as to the references.[4]

[Standard EDb-401-02(0)] means that a private school, a non-tax supported school is effectively under the control of the local board of education for all activities of the school.[5]

Putting myself in the place of a school administrator, it seems to me to pose very difficult problems [on how to go about opening a school].[6]

I find so many, many basic apparent inconsistencies in the document.[7]

In other words, it appears to me the State is saying, you may tell us what your school will be about through the statement of philosophy and purposes . . . but unless it conforms to these guidelines, you may not be approved.[8]

Going further, I find difficulty in places defining whether or not certain standards are applicable.[9]

Now, turning to some specific other standards, the question of [teacher] certification. . . .

My work with the non-public schools, and with this Massachusetts teacher certification Advisory Commission, and experience in reading, and so on, leads me to the conclusion that for non-public schools, non-tax supported schools, there is a severe question on both education and other grounds for the necessity for certification as a qualification for hiring a person as a teacher in one of these schools.

Each non-public school is one with certain basic philosophies and purposes. They cater to people who have certain educational interest [sic] for their children.

And really what the school needs more is a person with a unique educational background, and that type of person, certification, it seems to me, may be very, very useful for purposes of public education.

But for the purposes of non-public education raises severe questions about it, and I see nothing in the work I have done to indicate otherwise.

For example, a teacher with all of the credentials in the world may be superb in one school situation, and terrible in another.[10]

Turning to Physical Facilities. . . . A fundamental question here, I think is, what legitimate interest have the State in this area? . . . There is not a question in my mind the fact that the State has a legitimate interest in the public safety of the youngster in the school.

I question severely how much further beyond that it has to go in a non-tax supported school.

Some of the particular standards follow in the Level 1 area. Beyond that, I think are interesting in terms of the tremendous financial load, capital costs imposed on the school. . . .[11]

Question by Attorney Ball: Do the minimum standards with respect to which you have testified, and considering that they are required to be applied without exceptions, do they represent an interest which is a vital interest in education for a State to achieve?

West: I think they are an over-extension of the vital interest of a State in non-public schools.[12]

Question by the prosecuting attorney, Lee Fry: Do you have minimum standards in your New England Association?

West: Yes, sir.

Fry: Are they not similar?

West: No, sir. No way.[13]

Question by attorney Ball: In your expert opinion would it be a matter of compelling State interest that a school observe, a nonpublic school in Ohio, observe each of the minimum standards?

West: No.

Ball: The answer is, no?

West, No, sir.

Ball: Thank you. No more questions, Your Honor.[14]

TESTIMONY OF DR. DONALD ARTHUR ERICKSON

Dr. Donald Erickson, of Park Forest, Illinois, is a Professor of Education and Director of the Mid-West Administration Center at the University of Chicago. Holding a B.A. in religion and English from the Bob Jones University and a Ph.D. in administration from the University of Chicago, he had taught educational courses at the University of Chicago for eleven years at the time he testified in the trial. He had also taught one year at the Florida State University, and had conducted consultantship and research work for numerous private organizations and governmental bodies.

The list of educational organizations to which he belongs is impressive: Life member of the American Association of School Administrators, member of the National Organization for Legal Problems in Education, Phi Beta Kappa, the American Association of University Professors, and the American Education Research Association. He has published six research polygraph booklets, about fifty-five articles, and one book. His book, published by the University of Chicago Press, is a book on public controls for nonpublic schools, which subject was certainly germane to this trial. Dr. Erickson's central scholarly interests have been in the area of nonpublic education, particularly in the area of "what controls should be imposed upon non-public schools, either with support, or in the absence of support." He has also done extensive work on how to organize schools for optimum effectiveness, and how administrators should be trained and selected.[15]

The following statements are Dr. Erickson's responses, made under oath, to questions asked him concerning the Ohio Minimum Standards.

> Question by defense attorney Ball: Now, I would like to ask you as an expert to express your general conclusion with respect to the minimum standards?
>
> Erickson: I think the most important thing to say is that one does not have to choose between regulations and no regulations of non-public schools as different kinds of regulations are possible.
>
> And I am of the firm position that the State has some far-reaching fundamental educational responsibilities [sic].
>
> In other words, that it must regulate in education. However, I am also firmly convinced that the State can fulfill all its fundamental responsibilities in education without prescribing how people must be educated; where they must be educated; what kind of buildings they must be educated in; what must be in the program, and what must be the nature of the individual who instructs them.
>
> I call the kind of regulations as a short-hand term, that I think it is clearly represented in the Ohio minimum standards program, in that it attempts to, as I see it, to fulfill the State's responsibilities in education, but does so by dictating what the program must look like.
>
> And that is my fundamental objection to it. As I say, State regulations of non-public schools can fulfill the State responsibility without being at all as pragmatic as I consider the Ohio statutes, Ohio minimum standards to be.
>
> And if you like I could give you some reasons why I think the pragmatic thrust in regulations of non-public schools is educationally indefensible.
>
> Ball: Is educationally what, sir?

Erickson: Indefensible.

Ball: Would you please expand on that for the Court?

Erickson: Yes. I see four dangers in this. One, is that as I read the Ohio minimum standards, I guess I should put in parentheses, Your Honor, that I am vastly confused by these standards, and I don't know how I would advise a school administrator to proceed on the basis of that document.

But taking it at its face value, it seems to me to go a long way down the road toward obliterating any distinction between public and private education.

In other words, if the State says to me, you may run a private school because that is constitutionally all right, and then proceeds to tell me what that school must look like; who I may hire; and what the program must be; I am inclined to respond that is a meaningless freedom as far as I am concerned. . . .[16]

Now, obviously the public schools are schools operated by the State. They belong to the State in Ohio. The State has the right to run them the way it wishes.

The State has a right in public schools to dictate that the water fountain shall have a stream come out on an angle as this [the Minimum Standards] does.

It has the right to dictate that all teachers shall be certified; . . . .

Consequently, I think it is arbitrary, and a distinct infringement on my freedom as an educator if I am running a private school, in effect [making it] a public school.

This is my first objection.

My second objection, I think is more fundamental, and this is the one I think disturbs me the most. In that as I read the Ohio minimum standards, they begin by saying a school should be judged by its statement of philosophy in the light of its own objectives, and requires as a matter of fact the school to enunciate its objectives.

And then proceed to lay out a basis of education of that, that is founded upon a particular philosophy that State officials hold.

It is not at all, as I view it, a neutral document. And I would point particularly to the passages on the social studies.

If they don't enunciate an educational philosophy on social studies, then I have no idea what, and I have no hesitation in identifying that philosophy that is spelled out here as a secular humanism philosophy.

What I am saying, is that in my view the minimum

standards say that the school has a right to run its program in terms of its own philosophy, and then imposes upon the school a philosophy not only in terms of that statement concerning the social studies, and health, and other statements, but in terms of what we call a hidden curriculum. . . .[17]

I do believe that these standards, if, as I say are taken at face value, and enforced in effect take away from the school the right to run its philosophy.

If the standards do not represent a philosophy, what do they represent? They obviously represent some view of the good life, and how the children are to be prepared for it, and if that is to be decided by the State, fine.

If that and democracy is to be decided by the parents, I am afraid with all due respects for the good people who put that together, I view it as a mistake, the entire document as a whole.[18]

Dr. Erickson's third point deals with the idea of trying to make all the schools just like each other, which he calls "conventionality." "I think," he says, "there is a lot of evidence. . .that our schools today are pretty ineffective."[19]

I would also point out to some schools that I have studied carefully, Hebrew day schools in Chicago and elsewhere, that devote at least 50 per cent [sic] of the time to Hebrew studies, and then turn to the secular subjects, and out pace [sic] all the schools in the State in terms of the honors that their students win.

What I am saying, that as a professor of education, I view that prescription as very close to nonsense.[20]

There is quite a bit in the minimum standards on school size, class size, prescribed in terms of the number of pupils that must be in a school, and I would say that, that was supportable twenty years ago in terms of educational, but it is not supportable today.

The tendency of research today is to show that our schools are too big, not too small, and that is what is wrong with schools, among other things.

They have become too massive, and bureaucratic, and dehumanized, so that children cannot relate properly to teachers, and teachers cannot relate properly to each other.[21]

I would like to speak on just one more point. . . .The teacher certification issue. I would as a professor of education, say that there is probably no aspect of education that has been criticized more cogently than this.

Teacher certification standards often would prohibit an Einstein from teaching a class in mathematics. Would probably prohibit a Leonard Bernstein from teaching a class in music.

I would say, however, that in public education it is probably a necessary evil, because public education is a massive enterprise.

We have to have some way of sorting people out so we will try to improve the certification standards, as we are trying to do, but why impose them upon non-public schools.

. . . In so far as I know, there are only six States in the Union that require teachers certification of non-public schools.[22]

I think my fourth major objection to the minimum standards is, I think they are about the weakest way I know of to try to accomplish what they are designed to accomplish, and that is to make schools better.

My problem here is that I am afraid that matters of buildings and teacher certification and curriculum and what not, are so external to the teaching, learning encounter, that they don't get to the heart of the issue.

And I myself, could take you to many schools that are approved under standards like this, that I would characterize as among the worst schools in the world.

I am afraid that this is not in my mind an effective way to separate between the poor schools and the good schools.

What bothers me in this connection, first is that I talk to many parents who are quite content to send their children to a conventional school, and do absolutely nothing to back them up, and to back up the school to make the home a proper environment for learning.

These standards won't prosecute those parents, won't lead to the prosecution of those parents. But I have seen many examples in State standards used to prosecute parents who want to go the extra mile, do something extra for their students, but happen to do it in an unconventional way.

As an educator I find that indefensible.[23]

Question by defense attorney Ball: Doctor Erickson, did you hear my question at the conclusion of my redirect examination of Mr. West, as to whether these standards in your expert view, represent a compelling State interest?

Erickson: Yes, I did.

Ball: What would be your answer to that question?

Erickson: I want to answer that question as accurately as I can. Let me try, go at it this way, by saying, that I think it is fairly obvious that the standards represent an effort to meet the States [sic] responsibilities in education, but I view it as misdirected, ill-advised effort, and that I don't think the State has any compelling interest at all in requiring schools to live up to the minimum standards in this book as a whole.

Ball: Thank you. No more questions, Your Honor.[24]

SUMMARY

Although Christian Schools of Ohio does not endorse all the views of these educators, we find their testimony to be most helpful in expressing the truth that there is room for divergence in the field of education. The State does not have a unique grasp of the only way of education, but by promulgating a document such as the Minimum Standards the state acts as though it were the sole possessor of educational truth. Dr. R. J. Rushdoony has provided a summary for this chapter by writing of the institutional effect of the public schools of our day:

> The public school is a substitute institution for the Holy Roman Empire and the Roman Catholic Church of the middle ages and is a thoroughly medieval concept. A single culture is demanded, and the public school must create it. . . .[25]

That seems to be the sentiment expressed by these expert educators. We might paraphrase the thought to say: A single culture is demanded by the Minimum Standards, and the Minimum Standards, if they are not contested, must eventually create just such a medieval culture.

The experts have argued for our contentions that the Minimum Standards are a faulty document. They are vague, confusing, and arbitrary, in the words of the educators. Besides that they are dangerous to the concerns of educational freedom. They give to the state too much control over that which it has no proper authority to control. They are, in the words of Dr. Erickson, "educationally indefensible."

[1]*Ohio* v. *Whisner*, 47 Ohio St. 2d 181, 215 (1976).

[2]Transcript of Testimony, pp. 207-215, *Ohio* v. *Whisner*, 47 Ohio St. 2d 181 (1976).

[3]Ibid., p. 215.
[4]Ibid., p. 216.
[5]Ibid.
[6]Ibid., p. 217.
[7]Ibid., p. 218.
[8]Ibid., p. 220.
[9]Ibid.
[10]Ibid., pp. 222-223.
[11]Ibid., pp. 226-227.
[12]Ibid., p. 229.
[13]Ibid., p. 238.
[14]Ibid., p. 247.
[15]Ibid., pp. 254-257.
[16]Ibid., pp. 258-260.
[17]Ibid., pp. 260-262.
[18]Ibid., p. 263.
[19]Ibid., p. 264.
[20]Ibid., p. 265.
[21]Ibid., p. 266.
[22]Ibid., p. 267.
[23]Ibid., pp. 268-269.
[24]Ibid., pp. 269-270.
[25]Rousas J. Rushdoony, *Intellectual Schizophrenia*, (Philadelphia: The Presbyterian and Reformed Publishing Co., 1974), p. 50.

3

Levi Whisner's Religious Objections to the Minimum Standards

We have considered some of the educational objections to the Ohio Minimum Standards which were raised by expert witnesses in the *Whisner* trial. In this chapter we shall review the religious objections to the Minimum Standards as enunciated by Reverend Whisner on behalf of himself and the other parents who shared his criminal charges. Rather than to explore Pastor Whisner's comments in detail we will present the thrust of his objections as summarized by the Supreme Court of Ohio, and we will also examine the opinion of that Court as to the validity of those objections. In following this proposed plan for review of these objections we must of necessity reproduce an extensive quantity of legal language. While this may prove tedious for some, we are certain that the fundamental importance of the matter, coupled with the deep interest of Bible-believing Christians in understanding these concerns will adequately reward those who exert the time and concentration required for the perusal of these pages.

Our plan for the consideration of each of the objectionable minimum standards will be to examine 1) the standard itself, 2) the summary of Reverend Whisner's objection as written by the Court, and 3) the opinion of the Court as to the validity of the objections raised.

OBJECTIONS IN THE MINIMUM STANDARDS *PER SE*

The following material is cited from the majority opinion of the Ohio Supreme Court in the case *Ohio* v. *Whisner.*

Through the testimony of Rev. Whisner, appellants voiced religious objections to four of the state's denominated "minimum standards." Those standards, and appellants' [appellants in this trial were Rev. Whisner and his co-defendants] objections thereto, are set forth herein as follows:

1. EDb-401-02 (E) (6) — [pp. 6 and 24 of the Standards] — "A charter shall be granted after an inspection which determines that all standards have been met."[1]

Summary of objection: (Appellants do not desire a charter, because acceptance of same would constitute their agreement to comply with all standards, and thereby effectively remove their ability to control the direction of the school by reposing vast powers in the hands of the state.)[2]

[Note: page 24 of the Minimum Standards says that "A charter is issued only after an inspection by State Department personnel determines that *all* Ohio Minimum Elementary School Standards are met." (Emphasis ours)]

Opinion of the Court: It must be remembered that one of the "minimum standards" requires compliance with all such standards before a charter can be granted. See EDb-401-02(E)(6). This is so despite the fact that the statutes upon which the "minimum standards" are based, R.C. 3301.07 and 3301.16, do not expressly require such absolute compliance.

Moreover, certain of the "minimum standards" at least indirectly hamper the right of appellants to freely exercise their religious beliefs through the medium of the educational institution they have established expressly for that purpose.[3]

2. EDb-401-02(G) — [Minimum Standards, p. 6] — "Based on a minimum five-hour school day or one of greater length, the total instructional time allocation per week shall be:

"four-fifths — language arts, mathematics, social

studies, science, health, citizenship, related directed study and self-help; optional foreign language.

"one-fifth — directed physical education, music, art, special activities and optional applied arts." [Footnotes deleted][4]

Summary of objection: (Appellants complain that this standard does not expressly allot time in which Biblical and spiritual training may be given, and, in that it severely restricts the ability of the school to incorporate its religious teachings.)[5]

Opinion of the Court: We refer, first, to EDb-401-02(G), which allocates instructional time in the comprehensive curriculum required by R.C. 3313.60, almost to the minute. Since R.C. 3313.48 requires a minimum school day of five hours, the requirement of EDb-401-02(G) invariably results in further control of the educational policies of a non-public religious school in a manner that we cannot say is compelled by the enabling legislation pursuant to which the "minimum standards" were adopted. R.C. 3313.48 and 3313.60, although requiring a school day of defined length and effectively controlling the courses of study taught non-public school children, do not further impede the ability of a religious school to incorporate the tenets of its particular faith into its required courses. We think that EDb-401-02(G) "unduly burdens the free exercise of religion" and interferes "with the rights of conscience," by requiring a set amount of time to be devoted to subjects which, by their very nature, may not easily lend themselves to the teaching of religious principles (e.g. mathematics). We do not mean to imply that the subjects contained within EDb-401-02(G), or those contained within R.C. 3313.60, are not helpful in preparing non-public, as well as public, school children for the obligations which will eventually arise in the process of maturing into adulthood. We only emphasize that the reasonableness of the requirements contained within "minimum standard" EDb-401-02(G) wanes in the face of an attack premised upon a violation of the constitutional right of appellants to the free exercise of their chosen religion. [Footnotes deleted][6]

3. EDb-401-02(0) — [Minimum Standards, p. 7] — ". . .All activities shall conform to policies adopted by the board of education."

Summary of objection: (The contention is advanced by appellants that this standard virtually provides a blank check to the public authorities to control the entire operation of their school.)[7]

Opinion of the Court: Secondly, in our view, EDb-401-02(0), which requires "all activities" of a non-public school to conform to policies adopted by the board of education, plainly violates appellants' right to the free exercise of their religion. If the state is to discharge its duty of remaining strictly neutral, pursuant to the establishment clause of the First Amendment, with respect to religion, how can the state constitutionally require *all activities* of a non-public religious school, which, of necessity, must include *religious activities,* to conform to the policies of a purportedly "neutral" board? As stated long ago in *Bd. of Edn.* v. *Minor* (1872), 23 Ohio St. 211, 249-251:

". . . The state can have no religious opinions; and if it undertakes to enforce the teaching of such opinions, they must be the opinions of some natural person, or class of persons. If it embarks in this business, whose opinion shall it adopt? . . . .

". . . .But the real question here is, not what is the best religion, but how shall this best religion be secured? *I answer, it can best be secured by adopting the doctrine of this 7th section in our own bill of rights, and which I summarize in two words, by calling it the doctrine of 'hands off.'* Let the state not only keep its own hands off, but let it also see to it that religious sects keep their hands off each other. . . . This is the golden truth which it has taken the world eighteen centuries to learn, and which has at last solved the terrible enigma of 'church and state.' Among the many forms of stating this truth, as a principle of government, to my mind it is nowhere more fairly and beautifully set forth than in our own constitution. Were it in my power, I would not alter a syllable of the form in which it is there put down. It is the true republican doctrine. It is simple and easily understood. It means a free conflict of opinions as to things divine; and *it means masterly inactivity on the part of the state* except for the purpose of keeping the conflict [the spiritual conflict between the various religious groups] free, and preventing the violation of private rights or of the public peace. Meantime, the state will impartially aid all parties in their struggles after religious truth, by providing means for the increase of general knowledge, which is the handmaid of good government, as well as the true religion and morality. *It means that a man's right to his own religious convictions, and to impart them to his own children, and his and their right to engage, in conformity thereto, in harmless acts of worship toward the Almighty, are as sacred in the eye of the law as his rights of person or property, and that although in the minority, he shall be protected in the full and unrestricted enjoyment thereof. . . .*" [Emphasis added by the Court]

Although this passage has been modified to some extent in recent years with regard to the responsibilities of the state in the area of non-public education, . . . it contains continued vitality, nonetheless, *as an accurate expression of the necessary distinction between church and state, and as a perpetual warning of the potential pitfalls awaiting unreasonable and excessive state involvement in matters touching upon convictions of conscience.* [Emphasis ours].

Viewed in the above light, the inconsistency inherent in EDb-401-02(0), and the *concomitant unconstitutional interference with, and infringement upon, appellants' rights to freely pursue their religious beliefs, is apparent to a majority of this court.* [Emphasis ours][8]

4. EDb-401-07 — [Minimum Standards, p. 13] — "Efforts toward providing quality education by the school for the community it serves shall be achieved through cooperation and interaction between the school and the community. The understanding of the roles of each and a flow of information are basic to this relationship.

"(A) The elementary principal and staff in keeping with administrative or board of education policies shall provide evidence, through written materials and informational meetings, of a continuous effort to give professional interpretation of the school's policies, program, purposes, planning, strengths and needs.

"(B) Each elementary school shall demonstrate, through school-community activities, evidence of cooperative assessment of community needs to determine the purposes, program and planning for future educational improvement."

Summary of objection: (Appellants maintain that a Christian school cannot seek its direction from the world or from the community it serves.)[9]

Opinion of the Court: Finally, EDb-401-07(B), which requires a non-public religious school to cooperate with elements of the community in which it exists, infringes

> upon the rights of these appellants, consistent with their religious beliefs, to engage in complete, or nearly complete, separation from community affairs. As Rev. Whisner testified, these appellants religiously adhere to the literal Biblical command that they "[B]e not conformed to this world . . ." Upon the face of the record before us, the state may not require the contrary.
>
> In the light of the foregoing, we conclude that appellants have sustained their burden of establishing that the "minimum standards" infringe upon the right guaranteed them by the First Amendment to the Constitution of the United States, and by Section 7, Article I of the Ohio Constitution, to the free exercise of their religion.[10]

The four standards cited above comprise the basis of Pastor Whisner's religious convictions against the minimum standards *per se,* that is, the standards published in pages one through fifteen of the Minimum Standards publication. Because of these standards the Tabernacle Christian School did not want, would not seek, and could not accept a charter from the Ohio Department of Education. The Ohio Supreme Court, as we have seen, recognized the religious conflict represented by these standards and found in these objections sufficient grounds to sustain the defense.

Levi Whisner's objections to the Minimum Standards, however, do not end at page fifteen of the document; they are extensively augmented by the portion of the Minimum Standards beginning at page seventeen and presented as the "Interpretative and Explanatory Information" section. Let us now consider these further objections.

Objections to the Interpretative Section

The Interpretative Section is by far the larger of the two divisions of the Minimum Standards, extending from page seventeen through page one hundred twenty-eight. Within this section of the Standards are contained both the "Level I" and "Level II" requirements for chartering schools and suggestions for development beyond the minimum standards, respectively. This portion of the publication also lays out a philosophy of education for each major subject in the required curriculum.

To consider Pastor Whisner's religious objections to this section of the Minimum Standards, we may follow a procedure only slightly changed from that used to review the prior section. We shall consider 1) the prescriptive statement from the standards, and 2) the Ohio Supreme Court's summary of Pastor Whisner's objection. After considering four standards and four objections we shall consider the Court's opinion of all the objections raised in this section. The four objections to the interpretative section are listed below:

1. EDb-401-02(J) — "When a pupil transfers, within a school system or moves to a school outside of the school system, pertinent pupil information is forwarded to the principal of the receiving school. Office records of this nature are not released to parents and guardians. . . ."[11]

Summary of objection: (Appellants contend that it is very important for a parent to be appraised of everything occurring in school relating to his or her child or children.)[12]

2. EDb-401-03(B) [Minimum Standards, p. 30] — "1. Common problems are solved through the consensus of thinking and action of individuals in the group.

"2. Individuals have a responsibility of authentic citizenship as a member of the school, community, state, nation and world.

"3. Citizens have a responsibility for the welfare of others and for being willing to sacrifice for the common good."[13]

Summary of objection: (Appellants reject the idea that common problems are solved solely by the group, because they instead adhere to the belief that problems are solved by the group on their knees. In addition, appellants contend that these comments reflect a philosophy of "secular humanism" on the part of the state — a philosophy to which appellants cannot, consistent with their religious beliefs, ascribe.)[14]

3. EDb-401-03(B) (page 48) — "Organized group life of all types must act in accordance with established rules of social relationships and a system of social controls."[15]

Summary of the objection: (Appellants again object to the "humanism" philosophy allegedly espoused herein.)[16]

4. EDb-401-03(B) (page 60) — "The health of the child is perhaps the greatest single factor in the development of a well-rounded personality. . . . Its place in the curriculum becomes increasingly important as automation, population growth, changing moral standards and values, mounting pressures, and other changes in our society create new or intensify existing health problems. [Dele-

tion ours — this material is considered subsequently herein][17]

Summary of the objection: (Appellants contend that although man's standards may change with respect to moral values, God's does [*sic*] not.)[18]

The Ohio Supreme Court's opinion on the foregoing objections is as follows:

Our review of the particular "minimum standards" objected to by appellants discloses that the language utilized in those standards is facially neutral. . . .

However, as required by *Wisconsin* v. *Yoder* . . . we must also determine whether [a] regulation neutral on its face may, in its application, nonetheless offend the constitutional requirement for governmental neutrality . . . [because] it unduly burdens the free exercise of religion." . . . .

In this regard, we must conclude that the compendium of "minimum standards" promulgated by the State Board of Education, taken as a whole, "unduly burdens the free exercise of [appellants'] religion." *Wisconsin* v. *Yoder, supra.*[19] . . . .

There is an additional, independent reason, ignored by the lower courts in this case, that compels upholding appellants' attack upon the state's "minimum standards." In our view, these standards are so pervasive and all-encompassing that total compliance with each and every standard by a non-public school would effectively eradicate the distinction between public and non-public education, and thereby deprive these appellants of their traditional interest as parents to direct the upbringing and education of their children.[20] . . . .

The "minimum standards" under attack herein effectively repose power in the state Department of Education to control the essential elements of non-public education in this state. The expert testimony received in this regard unequivocably demonstrates the absolute suffocation of independent thought and educational policy, and the effective retardation of religious philosophy engendered by application of these "minimum standards" to non-public educational institutions.[21]

THE RELIGION OF LEVI WHISNER ET AL.

As we have now seen, the Ohio Supreme Court has ruled that

the Ohio Minimum Standards violate the religious free exercise of Rev. Levi Whisner and his co-defendants. It is therefore important that we understand exactly what "religion" was adhered to by these former criminals. Here is the Court's summary of the religious description of Pastor Whisner and his co-defendants:

> Based on the extensive record before us, there can be no doubt but that appellants' religious beliefs are "truly held." Rev. Whisner's testimony clearly reveals that the religion in which he believes is a historical religion consisting of "born-again" Christians, who adhere to a life of separation from worldliness, and who strictly structure their lives upon a subjective interpretation of Biblical language. The uncontradicted testimony of Rev. Whisner, and that of the other defense witnesses, as documented in the foregoing statement of the case, conclusively establishes that these appellants are God-fearing people with an abiding religious conviction that Biblical training is essential to the proper inculcation of spiritual and moral values into their youth at a time when such precepts are most likely to take root — during the formative years of educational growth and physical development. In this regard, appellants' testimony unmistakenly emphasizes their collective dissatisfaction with the form of the education provided by the public schools of this state, and their total religious compulsion that their offspring be educated in the Word of God according to their religious scruples. Moreover, the sincerity of appellants' religious beliefs can best be illustrated by the very fact that they were willing to subject themselves to the criminal process of this state in order to vindicate their position. No more need be said concerning the sincerity of appellants' religious beliefs, for, in our view, it has been established beyond peradventure.[22]

Such a description might have been applied to other religious criminals of the past, such as the apostles Peter and Paul, who also felt the effects and endured the punishments of laws which were violative of the free exercise of their religion. Virtually the same religious convictions form the foundation for all of the Bible-believing Christian schools in this state and in other states, and these convictions are shared by parents throughout the state and the nation. The opinion of the Ohio Supreme Court, therefore, carries a message to all the Bible-believing Christians in the State — and to many who live in other states.

SUMMARY

The justices of the Ohio Supreme Court have carefully studied the religious objections of Rev. Whisner and his co-defendants which prohibited the compliance of their school with the Ohio Minimum Standards. This study has vindicated the religious liberty struggle of these parents who send their children to a small, independent, church-operated Christian school in Bradford, Ohio.

In the course of the *Whisner* opinion the Court has mentioned that the Ohio Minimum Standards, as applied to the Tabernacle Christian School (and by implication, to other church-operated Christian schools in Ohio whose supporters share the convictions of Whisner et al.) are violative of the First and Fourteenth Amendments to the U.S. Constitution and of Article I, section 7, of the Ohio Constitution. The Court has also stated that the Minimum Standards deprive parents of their traditional interest "to direct the upbringing and education of their children." The Standards are seen as overly-demanding to the extent of eradicating "the distinction between public and nonpublic education," and they are said to be absolutely suffocating to both "independent thought and educational policy," and to be retardant to "religious philosophy." Other than that, it appears, the Standards are all right.

[1]*Ohio* v. *Whisner,* 47 Ohio St. 2d 181 (1976), at p. 201.

[2]Ibid.

[3]Ibid., pp. 204, 205.

[4]Ibid., p. 201.

[5]Ibid.

[6]Ibid., pp. 206, 207.

[7]Ibid., p. 201.

[8]Ibid., pp. 207-209.

[9]Ibid., p. 202.

[10]Ibid., pp. 209, 210.

[11]Ibid., p. 202.

[12]Ibid.

[13]Ibid.

[14]Ibid., pp. 202, 203.

[15]Ibid., p. 203.

[16]Ibid.

[17]Ibid.

[18]Ibid.

[19]Ibid., pp. 203, 204.

[20]Ibid., pp. 211, 212.

[21]Ibid., p. 215.

[22]Ibid., pp. 199, 200.

4
The Philosophy of the Minimum Standards: The Establishment of a State Religion

We read in the Amendments to the Constitution of the United States that:

> Congress shall make no law respecting an establishment of religion, or prohibiting the free exercise thereof. . . .[1]

The Constitution further provides that:

> . . . . No State shall make or enforce any law which shall abridge the privileges or immunities of citizens of the United States. . . .[2]

The First Amendment to the Constitution of the United States of America contains two clauses intended to limit the Federal government for the protection of the religious liberty of America's citizenry. The clauses are known as the "Establishment Clause" and the "Free Exercise Clause." The Establishment Clause prohibits the Federal Congress from choosing or "establishing" a state religion. It also prevents the Congress from giving favorable treatment to any specific religious group, as by funding or special privileges. The Free Exercise

Clause guarantees to citizens the right to practice or "exercise" their religious beliefs as they deem proper. Subsequent case law has determined that this right is not absolute; a man cannot infringe upon the rights of others and protect such practices by claiming the protection of the Free Exercise Clause. But the courts of our land have consistently upheld the right of a man to the enjoyment of such religious worship and activities as derive from his religious convictions and are not harmful to the rights of others.

The Fourteenth Amendment, enacted subsequent to the Civil War, extends to the several state governments the same limitations as are imposed upon the Federal Government. A liberty, therefore, which is guaranteed by the U. S. Constitution may not be violated by the laws of any state government.

On July 28, 1976, the Ohio Supreme Court ruled that the Ohio Minimum Standards (for elementary schools) violate the freedom of religion guarantees of the First and Fourteenth Amendments to the U. S. Constitution, as these Standards are applied to church-related (or church-operated) schools. Ohio's High Court recognized that the Minimum Standards are violative of the First Amendment right to the "free exercise of religion." This judgment was given as the criminal convictions of Rev. Levi Whisner and his co-defendants were reversed.

We have seen in the previous chapter how the Minimum Standards are violative of the Free Exercise Clause of the Constitution. The Whisner case, however, as crucial as it was, did not approach the Minimum Standards as a violation of the Establishment Clause of the First Amendment. We must realize that the periphery of this subject was broached, but clearly the Establishment Clause was not presented as an issue of the case. Since it was not an issue in the Whisner case, the Ohio Supreme Court did not rule on it. This fact leaves the "Establishment" question unresolved, and it is a question of fundamental importance to all Bible-believing Christians.

The "establishment of religion" question with respect to the Ohio Minimum Standards must be resolved, for many citizens believe that the philosophy of education spelled out in the Ohio Minimum Standards is indeed an "establishment of religion," that is, a state religion. If this be true, the Ohio Minimum Standards are unconstitutional not only as applied to church-related schools, but also as applied to every school in the state. The Standards then violate the First Amendment rights of every school child, every parent, every taxpayer, and, indeed, of every citizen in the State of Ohio.

CSO views the educational philosophy of the Minimum Standards as an establishment of religion. To adequately consider the evidence for this allegation we must take the following steps: 1) identify the philosophy of the Minimum Standards, 2) show that it is a religion, 3) examine the religion involved, and 4) see how the Minimum Standards espouse and promulgate this religion. We shall attempt to carry out steps 1) and 2) in this chapter, and shall pursue the investigation of steps 3) and 4) in ensuing chapters.

Identifying the Philosophy of the Minimum Standards

Because the philosophy sections of the Minimum Standards deal with an educational philosophy, an identification of the philosophy should ideally be made by an expert educator. Such an identification is available. It was made in the courtroom, under oath, by a highly qualified and recognized educational expert.

Dr. Donald Erickson, whose credentials and testimony in the Whisner trial appeared earlier, clearly labeled the Minimum Standards' philosophy as a philosophy of "Secular Humanism." Again quoting from the transcript of testimony of the *Whisner* trial, we have Dr. Erickson's exact statement: ". . .and I have no hesitation in identifying that philosophy that is spelled out here as a secular humanism philosophy."[3] Dr. Erickson was referring specifically to the philosophy of social studies which is presented in the Minimum Standards on pages 47-49, but the philosophy of Secular Humanism pervades the Minimum Standards, as we shall see hereafter.

The majority opinion of the Ohio Supreme Court in the *Whisner* case corroborates Dr. Erickson's identification. Even though the justices did not rule on the establishment of religion issue they did express concern over the Humanism espoused in the Minimum Standards. The Court emphasized the correctness of Dr. Erickson's identification of the Minimum Standards' philosophy as one of Secular Humanism in this cautiously worded statement:

> In this regard, we share the concern of appellants [*Whisner* et al.] that the philosophy espoused especially in EDb-401-03(B), relating to the teaching of citizenship, social studies and health, may be interpreted as promoting "secular humanism," and, as such, may unconstitutionally be applied to these appellants to "unduly burden the free exercise of religion. . . ."[4]

The Court goes on to explain its cautious statement that the philosophy "may be interpreted as promoting 'secular humanism,' " by adding "should that section of the publication be interpreted as part of the 'minimum standards.' "[5]

But is the philosophy section to be interpreted as a part of the Minimum Standards? The Court does not give a final decision. Instead, the ruling informs us that "we do not decide that issue in this case. . . ."[6] We shall ponder the legal force of the "Interpretative Section" of the Minimum Standards in a later chapter, but at this point in our consideration we must take due notice of the manner in which the Court has supported the expert testimony of Dr. Erickson. Reviewing the pertinent portion of the Court's statement we find that "the [Minimum Standards'] philosophy . . . may be interpreted as promoting 'secular humanism. . . .' "[7]

The final and conclusive identification of the Minimum Standards philosophy as one of Secular Humanism must come after a thorough examination of the internal evidence in the philosophical statements themselves. It was from such an examination that Dr. Erickson and the Supreme Court justices drew their conclusions as to the identity of this philosophy. In a later chapter we shall compare the doctrinal and philosophical pronouncements of avowed Humanists with the philosophical statements in the Minimum Standards. We shall see that the two philosophies are identical, and we shall thereby underscore the conclusion of Dr. Erickson and the Ohio Supreme Court as to the identity of the philosophy in the Minimum Standards. It is undeniably one of Secular Humanism.

SECULAR HUMANISM: AN ANTI-CHRISTIAN RELIGION

But why express such concern over the philosophy of Secular Humanism and its inclusion in the Minimum Standards as a State-ordered philosophy of education? Simply this: **Secular Humanism is a religion!**

To prove that Secular Humanism is a religion is not difficult, for the evidence is plentiful. To make our consideration complete we must reflect upon 1) the dictionary definition of a religion, 2) the Humanists' analysis of their own beliefs, and 3) the opinion of the United States Supreme Court on Secular Humanism.

Religion Defined

The word "religion" normally evokes mental images of such accouterments as cathedrals, temples, churches, mitred prelates, parading popes, or pulpit-pounding preachers. For some the word brings thoughts of an open Bible, a weeping penitent, or a sawdust trail. The word itself may call forth any number of associations, dependent perhaps upon the background of the person who hears and responds to the word.

All of the religion-related thoughts in the previous paragraph are in some way associated with a belief in God, but the word "religion" does *not always* signify such a belief in a Supreme Being. There are some beliefs which are religious in nature even though they reject the particular tenet of a Supernatural Being. Such systems of belief are nevertheless religious because they deal with religious questions or issues.

The definition of "religion" supplied by the *American College Dictionary (ACD)* burrows to the heart of the matter and shows the underlying essentials of a religion. A religion, explains the *ACD*, is "the quest for the values of the ideal life, involving 3 phases: the ideal, the practices for attaining the values of the ideal, and the theology or world view relating the quest to the environing universe."[8]

Without excessive reflection upon this definition we see that a religion involves life values, life practices, and a world view. A man might easily embrace a systematic body of doctrine which both meets these criteria of religion and rejects belief in God. A man, therefore, who does not believe in God may nevertheless be religious and have religious beliefs.

Consider, for example, the religious belief that "there is a God." This belief is clearly a religious doctrine. If the opposite be affirmed, namely, "there is no God," such a doctrine may be labeled "atheistic," but it is, nevertheless, a religious belief. It deals with a religious question (the existence of God), it is a belief, and therefore it is a religious belief.

For these reasons, Secular Humanism is a religion. It is true that a *thoroughgoing* Humanist* scoffs at belief in God; he may never go to church (although this is not always the case, as we shall see), and he would never bow for prayer. Yet he does hold to a system of beliefs that defines his values in life; his values guide him in the practical decisions of daily living; and his values and decisions are structured upon a cosmology or world view that grows out of his religious presuppositions.

*It must be noted that there are various shades of belief among Humanists, just as there are various shades of belief among Protestants, Baptists, Catholics, and other religious groups. By "thoroughgoing Humanist" the author means one who adheres to a strict, logical progression of beliefs based on the Humanistic presuppositions. Not all Humanists are consistently Humanistic in their doctrines, just as not all Christians are consistently Scriptural in their beliefs.

Secular Humanism, then, meets the dictionary qualifications for a religion. As Dr. Rushdoony has stated this truth:

> It is perhaps necessary at this point to remind ourselves that it is a fallacy to think of religion as a belief in a personal God. To do so is to define all religions in Biblical terms and to impose the nature of one religion as definitive of all religions. Most religions, in fact, are not theistic.[9]

Let us move on to discover further evidence which requires that we regard the philosophy of Secular Humanism as a religion.

Humanists Claim Religious Status

Although some traditionally-minded folk may question the inclusion of Humanism among the world's religions, the Humanists themselves suffer from no such delusion. They have left no doubt as to their analysis of their own beliefs, and they adamantly declare the religious status of Humanism. A number of eminent Humanists signed a document published in 1933 and dubbed "A Humanist Manifesto." The purpose of this document was, as the name suggests, to codify and affirm the major doctrinal theses of their mutually-held faith. Listen in as the Humanists themselves argue for the acceptance of their convictions as a *bona fide* religion:

> The time has come for a widespread recognition of the radical changes in religious beliefs throughout the modern world. . . . In every field of human activity, the vital movement is now in the direction of a candid and explicit humanism. In order that religious humanism may be better understood we, the undersigned, desire to make certain affirmations which we believe the facts of our contemporary life demonstrate.
>
> There is a great danger of a final, and we believe fatal, identification of the word *religion* with doctrines and methods which have lost their significance and which are powerless to solve the problem of human living in the Twentieth Century. Religions have always been means for realizing the highest values of life. Their end has been accomplished through the interpretation of the total environing situation (theology or world view), the sense of values resulting therefrom (goal or ideal), and the technique (cult), established for realizing the satisfactory life. A change in any of these factors results in alteration of the outward forms of religion. . . .
>
> Today man's larger understanding of the universe, his scientific achievements, and his deeper appreciation of

> brotherhood, have created a situation which requires a new statement of the means and purposes of religion. Such a vital, fearless, and frank religion capable of furnishing adequate social goals and personal satisfactions may appear to many people as a complete break with the past. While this age does owe a vast debt to the traditional religions, it is none the less obvious that any religion that can hope to be a synthesizing and dynamic force for today must be shaped for the needs of this age. To establish such a religion is a major necessity of the present. It is a responsibility which rests upon this generation. . . .[10]

Then follow the fifteen "theses of religious humanism," as they are labeled by the authors. It is abundantly clear that the Humanists themselves regard their theses — their convictions, tenets, creeds, doctrines, or whatever — as a religion. Their stated purpose for setting pen to paper was to "establish . . . a religion" to meet "the needs of this age." Although the success of their man-made religion is open to question, the fact that these men have enunciated a systematic body of religious doctrine is clear beyond peradventure. Humanism is a religion, and the Humanists themselves were the first to "manifest" this fact.

Because our present interest in Humanism is generated by the educational philosophy apparently handed down as a bureaucratic fiat by the Ohio Department of Education, it is important that we here consider the contributions of a man who was both a renowned educator and an influential Humanist. This man is often referred to as the "father of progressive education," but is less often remembered as a signatory of the Humanist Manifesto of 1933, to which we have just referred. It is the well-known philosopher, writer, and educator, John Dewey of whom we now speak, and it is true that John Dewey joined thirty-three other Humanists in signing the 1933 Manifesto.

This single fact, perhaps, best illuminates Dewey's evangelistic zeal in the reformation of American education. As a Humanist — one dedicated to the establishment of a new religion which would function as a "synthesizing and dynamic force for today,"[11] Dewey recognized the vast potential offered by American public education as a vehicle for the propagation of his new faith. Both the writings of Dewey and the writings about Dewey point again and again to his *religious* impact on American *education*.

And John Dewey saw very incisively the hidden but smouldering force vested in a philosophy of education to effect the changes in society which could reshape America in the image of his (Dewey's) religion. John L. Childs, writing about Dewey's educational philosophy, points out that "a difference in philosophy which makes no difference in the practice of education is an artificial, or verbal, difference."[12] Childs continues by explaining:

> All deliberate education is thus, in his [Dewey's] opinion, a *moral* undertaking. Moral in the sense that it is a designed, controlled action concerned with the formation of fundamental attitudes of the individual toward nature and fellow human beings. It inescapably involves the manifestation of preference for some particular kind of social and individual life. [Emphasis his][13]

If, then, the intention of Dewey's philosophy was moral, and its aim was to alter the "formation of fundamental attitudes," did Dewey seek the alteration of religious attitudes? The answer is an unequivocal "Yes!" Mr. Childs states that Dewey's methodology (used in conjunction with his philosophy) is incompatible with a Christian philosophy of education. He explains it in this way:

> To be sure, the method as such does not automatically prescribe a complete set of metaphysical theses, but it does, nevertheless, define a principle of approach and analysis which clearly is not compatible with certain philosophical presuppositions. It inevitably cuts the ground, for example, from under the conception of supernaturalism. . . . From the standpoint of culture and education such a shift in general outlook carries consequences for human conduct and belief far too important to be subsumed under the category of method. A new world-view may be the necessary correlative of this empirical method. . . .[14]

A new world-view! More simply stated, a new *religion* was required if the methodology of Dr. Dewey were to be used. Which religion would be required? Why, Humanism, of course. Dr. Dewey saw education as the means of establishing his religion of Humanism as *the* religion of society.

Dewey, of course, was not bashful about his hopes for the alteration of society. One of his works, "My Pedagogic Creed," reveals the openly religious goals he sought in effecting social change:

> I believe that
> — the teacher is engaged, not simply in the training of individuals, but in the formation of the proper social life.
>
> — every teacher should realize the dignity of his call-

ing; that he is a social servant set apart for the maintenance of proper social order and the securing of the right social growth.

— in this way the teacher always is the prophet of the true God and the usherer in of the true kingdom of God.[15]

John Dewey is an important figure to consider as we reflect on the religious nature of Humanism. Although both Humanism and American education existed prior to John Dewey, it was during his lifetime that the two became one. That is not to say that the union was immediate and complete, for it was gradual. We might say it was progressive. Neither does this statement infer that the union of Humanism and American education was due solely to the influence of John Dewey, but certainly he served as a catalyst to speed up the process. Dewey the Humanist wrought great changes in the American philosophy of education, and those changes still affect (or afflict, depending on one's presuppositions) our nation today. The educators since Dewey, who have used Dewey's work as their launching pad, have expanded the implications of "progressive education" and steered a course toward a totally Humanistic educational system. The success of the progressive application of Humanism and Deweyism to American education may be judged, we believe, by the condition of the schools and students in our country today. Academic levels plunge, colleges lament, promiscuity abounds, vandalism soars, safety on school grounds and in the hallways diminishes, and the voters torpedo countless school levies. These ramifications of Humanism at work are not, however, the immediate subject of the present work. Since our daily newspapers abound in documentation for these fruits of Humanism, but rarely discover the root of the problem, we turn our thoughts back in that direction.

In 1973 a second Humanist Manifesto was written and sent forth to update the first Manifesto, which was then forty years old. Bible-believing Christians, who are accustomed to trusting a completed Revelation for their guidance, may deem it strange for men to update the tenets of their religion. Such a practice, however, is only to be expected. When men set out to establish a religion of their own, as the Humanists of 1933 claimed to do, they must accept the changes required for accommodation with a changing society.

The new Manifesto, though clearly a religious document, concentrated less on the Humanist claim to religious status than did the Humanist Manifesto I. Presumably that matter was considered settled, and the second Manifesto assumed the religious status of Humanism as an accepted fact. The writers of the new Manifesto felt free to concentrate on an attack of the "traditional" religions — particularly those that adhere to a belief in God, the Bible, and eternal salvation.

To demonstrate the religious nature of the Humanist Manifesto II, we will consider briefly only three items. First, the preface to the second Manifesto contains a confession for the need of faith on the part of practicing Humanists. An exhortation for believers to exercise faith in their religion is certainly to be expected in a religious document. Second, one of the major sections of the Manifesto reviews the Humanist conception of religion. It explains what religion is and is not, from the Humanist standpoint. Third, many of the other doctrines covered in the Humanist Manifesto II are religious in nature and thus confirm the religious thrust of the document. Because much of the content of this Manifesto is scrutinized in the next two chapters of this work, this brief précis of the internal religious orientation will suffice for now.

At this point let us summarize the evidence presented by the Humanists regarding the status of their beliefs. First, the Humanist Manifesto of 1933 argues strongly that Humanism is a religion. Second, John Dewey, who endorsed that document by signing it, exhibited clearly the religious nature of Humanism in the philosophical, methodological, and pedagogical teachings which he introduced into American public education. Finally, the Humanist Manifesto II of 1973 accepts the religious status of Humanism as a fact and launches an attack upon the "traditional" or theistic religions. Clearly, then, there can be no doubt that those who embrace the beliefs of Humanism count those beliefs a religion.

We have seen that the tenets of Humanism fit the dictionary definition of a religion and that the Humanists accord their views the standing of a religion. Now we must consider the legal position assigned to Humanism by our nation's highest tribunal.

The U. S. Supreme Court and Secular Humanism

The United States Supreme Court, in judging certain religious cases, has had to deal with the matter of Secular Humanism. The uncontradicted testimony of the Court is that Secular Humanism is a religion. In 1961, for instance, the Court ruled on the matter of *Torcaso* v. *Watkins.* Roy Torcaso complained that his First and Fourteenth Amendment rights under the Federal Constitution had been violated by a requirement of the Maryland Constitution which decreed that each person holding an office of public trust must profess belief in God. Since Torcaso did not believe in God, he argued that the requirement violated his freedom of religion. Now listen to a portion of the ruling of the Court as delivered by Justice Black:

> We repeat and again reaffirm that neither a State nor the Federal Government can constitutionally force a person "to profess a belief or disbelief in any religion." *Neither can constitutionally pass laws or impose requirements which aid all religions as against nonbelievers, and neither can aid those religions based on a belief in the existence of God as against those religions founded on different beliefs.* [Emphasis added][16]

Justice Black here points out that there are some religions which are "founded on different beliefs" than the belief in God. Because Justice Black realized that we might question this statement by asking "What religions are founded on such atheistic beliefs?" he placed a footnote at this point to illuminate his comment. It is footnote eleven, and it tells us:

> 11. *Among religions in this country* which do not teach what would generally be considered a belief in the existence of God *are* Buddhism, Taoism, Ethical Culture, *Secular Humanism* and others. . . . [Emphasis added][17]

Because this opinion represents the thinking of seven Supreme Court Justices, a substantial majority, we must view this case as a legal recognition by the highest Judicial Body of our land that Secular Humanism is indeed a religion.

Summary

Thus far in our inquiry we have discovered some startling evidence. There can be no reasonable question about the religious status of the philosophy of Secular Humanism. As we have seen, it complies with the dictionary definition of a religion, its own adherents claim that it is a religion, and the United States Supreme Court has recognized it as a religion. *Secular Humanism is a religion!*

The Ohio Minimum Standards, as we have also seen in this chapter, espouse an educational philosophy which has been identified in court by an educational expert witness as a "secular humanism philosophy."[18] The Ohio Supreme Court has expressed concern over the evident Secular Humanism of the Standards. We are surely headed for a conclusion that the State of Ohio, through the Ohio Department of Education, has indeed established a state religion in the schools of this state. If this is true, then the following are also true:

1. The Ohio Minimum Standards violate the First and Fourteenth Amendments to the United States Constitution. (The Ohio Supreme Court, in *Whisner,* has already ascertained this violation in the application of these standards to certain church-related schools. This *Whisner* decision, however, was made on the basis of the violation of the "Free Exercise Clause," but we are concerned in this chapter with the violation of the "Establishment Clause.")

2. The Minimum Standards violate the constitutional rights of every school-age child in the state by subjecting each one to a state-established religion.

3. The Minimum Standards violate the rights of every parent in the state to determine the religious upbringing of his children.

4. The Minimum Standards apparently violate the rights of every nonpublic school, including all church-operated schools, by imposing on such schools the requirement of compliance with a state religion, and

5. The Minimum Standards violate the rights of all the taxpayers in the state by using their tax revenues for the aid and propagation of a state religion in all of the elementary schools in the state.

Again, if it is true that the Ohio Department of Education has established a state religion in the elementary schools of our state, where young minds are plastic and easily influenced, it also follows that a threat to the very concept of freedom has been introduced into our state and nation.

We have now reached a point at which we must investigate more thoroughly the internal evidence of the Minimum Standards to see if this evidence supports Dr. Erickson's affirmation that the Mimimum Standards' philosophy is one of Secular Humanism. Before we begin this investigation, however, it will be necessary to first examine the cardinal doctrines of the religion of Secular Humanism.

[1]U. S. Const. amend. I.

[2]U. S. Const. amend. XIV, sec. 1.

[3]Transcript of Testimony, p. 262, *Ohio* v. *Whisner,* 47 Ohio St. 2d 181 (1976).

[4]*Ohio* v. *Whisner,* 47 Ohio St. 2d 181 (1976), at p. 211.

[5]Ibid.

[6]Ibid.

[7]Ibid.

[8]C. L. Barnhart et al. (eds.), *The American College Dictionary* (New York: Random House, 1964).

[9]Rousas John Rushdoony, "The State as an Establishment of Religion" (paper read at the Notre Dame University Law School symposium, April, 1976, Notre Dame, Indiana).

[10]Oliver Leslie Reiser, *Humanism and New World Ideals* (Yellow Springs, Ohio: Antioch Press, n.d.), pp. 43, 44.

[11]Ibid., p. 44.

[12]John L. Childs, "The Educational Philosophy of John Dewey," *The Philosophy of John Dewey*, ed. Paul Arthur Schilpp (New York: Tudor Publishing Co., 1951), p. 420.

[13]Ibid.

[14]Ibid., p. 421.

[15]John Dewey, *John Dewey on Education - Selected Writings*, ed. Reginald D. Archambault (New York: Random House, Inc., 1964), p. 439.

[16]*Torcaso* v. *Watkins,* 367 U.S. 488, 6 L ed 2d 982, 81 S Ct 1680 (1961), at 367 U.S. 495 and 6 L ed 2d 987.

[17]Ibid.

[18]*Whisner* Transcript of Testimony, op. cit., p. 262.

5

A Survey of the Religion of Secular Humanism

In the preceding chapter we have seen that the philosophy known as Secular Humanism is undeniably a religion. In the next chapter, i.e. chapter 6, we shall see how the doctrines of the religion of Secular Humanism are woven into the educational philosophy of the Ohio Minimum Standards. Before we undertake that assignment, however, it will be helpful to our consideration if we acquaint ourselves more fully with this atheistic religion by surveying 1) its name, 2) its history, 3) its manifestoes, 4) its cardinal doctrines, and 5) its treatment in the Bible. Tracing these lines of inquiry will prepare us for a full appreciation of the content in the vital chapter to follow.

SECULAR HUMANISM: THE NAME

Throughout this paper we have consistently capitalized both "Humanism" and "Secular Humanism," except when quoting other sources in which these names were given in the lower case. These names are often written without capitals, but in the light of the foregoing chapter this practice must be taken as incorrect. Because it is a standard English rule to capitalize the names of religions and denominations, as, for example, Catholicism or Buddhism, Baptist and Christian, "Secular Humanism" must also be capitalized, if merely to remind us that it is a religion.

We have also used the names "Humanism" and "Secular Humanism" interchangeably. The religion is probably best characterized by the longer appellation, "Secular Humanism." This denomination emphasizes the tenets and philosophy of *secularism,* which philosophy is defined as follows by *The Shorter Oxford English Dictionary on Historical Principles:*

> Secularism 1. The doctrine that morality should be based solely on regard to the well-being of mankind in the present life, to the exclusion of all considerations drawn from belief in God or in a future state.[1]

Although the adjective "secular" is commonly construed as synonymous with "non-religious" this meaning is incorrect in "*Secular* Humanism." As the definition above so clearly evinces, secularism is the exclusion of *God,* not *religion.* When the adjectival form is used with Humanism, "Secular" must be understood as promoting the exclusion of God rather than the absence of religion. Properly viewed, Secular Humanism is atheistic but not irreligious.

The Humanists themselves use the term "Secular" Humanism in neither of their published manifestoes, yet both of these documents teach Secular Humanism. The documents are entitled "A Humanist Manifesto" and "Humanist Manifesto II." These titles had probably been more accurate if the adjective "Secular" had been included. The term "Humanism" is actually broader than the manifestoes. It embraces many variations of humanistic thought, including that of the Renaissance Humanists, who were probably not as outspoken in their rejection of theism as are the twentieth-century Secular Humanists. According to *The New Columbia Encyclopedia:*

> . . . The term [humanist] was originally restricted to a point of view prevalent among thinkers in the Renaissance. The distinctive characteristics of Renaissance humanism were its emphasis on classical studies, or the humanities, and a conscious return to classical ideals and forms. The movement led to a restudy of the Scriptures and gave impetus to the Reformation [*sic*]. The term humanist is applied to such diverse men as Giovanni Boccaccio, Petrarch, Lorenzo Valla, Lorenzo dé Medici, Erasmus, and Thomas More.[2]

Despite the differences of thought which have been catalogued under the title of humanism by this statement, the Secular Humanists who wrote and signed the two Humanist Manifestoes referred to themselves merely as "humanists," or even, as we have noted above, as "religious humanists." It may be argued, on one hand, that the writers of the two Manifestoes ought to have identified their writings as "Secular Humanist Manifestoes," in order to more carefully identify their "denomination" among the various shades of Humanistic belief. On the other hand, the writers of these two documents have enunciated the presuppositions which underlie the very heart of Humanism (such as disbelief in God and in a revelation from God) and it may be argued that by so doing they have laid down in a clear and concise form *the* truly Humanistic doctrine. In this way then, these twentieth-century Humanists are correct in dropping the term "secular" from their name. Pure Humanism is unavoidably secular in character. Pure Humanism is also unavoidably religious in nature because of its concern with religious subjects, e.g. the existence of God, the goals of life, life values, morality, and so on. With these thoughts in mind we must regard "Humanism," "religious humanism," and "Secular Humanism" as synonymous. This seems strange since we commonly regard "religious" and "secular" as opposites. The paradox is resolved, however, in the following rule of thumb: Humanism is secular because it excludes God and religious because it deals with religious subjects.

In this work, then, the terms "Humanism," "religious Humanism," and "Secular Humanism" are used interchangeably. We believe this practice accords with the usage of the two Humanist Manifestoes and represents an accurate relationship as to the philosophy under consideration.

The History of Secular Humanism

Humanism, as we have already seen, became a popular belief during the Renaissance. The doctrines of the Humanists had been in existence long before that time, but it was during the Renaissance that the name "Humanism" came into use to identify these beliefs. The first Humanists, living in fourteenth-century Italy, derived the name from the Latin "*studia humanitatis,* or 'humanities,' which Roman authors had used in the sense of a liberal or literary education."[3] These students of antiquity, especially Greek and Roman antiquity, reintroduced the study of the classical authors, many of whom had been set aside "because of their disturbingly pagan quality. . . ."[4]

Indeed, the pagan culture of ancient Greece promoted many of the same ideas espoused by the Humanists of our day. The Greek philosophy of hedonism, for example, was a Humanistic philosophy which taught that "pleasure or happiness is the highest good."[5] Humanistic doctrine is abroad in our land today and is expressed in such popular maxims as "If it feels good — do it," and "Do your own thing."

The underlying theme in Humanism is and has always been the *autonomy* of man. Man as his own highest authority in all of life, man as his own reason for living, man as god — this is the basis of Humanism. By isolating this most basic presupposition of Humanism, namely, the deity of man, we can trace the religion back beyond the Golden Age of Greece, back into the antiquity of Bible times. The Bible, both in the Old and New Testaments, abounds with illustrations of the Humanistic rebellion of men against their God. The Apostle Paul is writing of the Humanist's view of life in Romans 1:25 when he describes those "Who changed the truth of God into a lie, and worshipped and served the creature more than the Creator, who is blessed for ever. Amen."

The Old Testament's King Nebuchadnezzar was a good example of a Humanist. He credited himself with the building of the mighty kingdom of Babylon until God humbled him. He was worshipping himself rather than God. Later in his life he repented and worshipped the Lord. Many similar examples could be mentioned, but we must hurry back to the beginning of things in the book of Genesis.

In the eleventh chapter of Genesis we find a group of Humanists who decided to build a city and a tower in order to make themselves a name. Here at the Tower of Babel men were intent upon the glorification (or worship) of themselves. The Lord confounded their plans and explained that if the people should remain in one place under a single government there would be no end to their wickedness. The Lord therefore confused their language and established the principle of nationalism. From that day to this Humanists have sought to do away with nationalism and replace it with a one-world government.

If we go all the way back to the third chapter of Genesis, we have the account of the first use of Humanism by the first humans. When Satan tempted Eve to disobey the clear command of God, he enticed her with a Humanistic appeal: "Ye shall be as gods, knowing good and evil."[6] The desire of man to be as God or to be his own god is as old as man himself.

But how did Satan know that the temptation of Humanism would be an effective means of drawing Adam and Eve into sin and rebellion against God? Was it not because Satan himself was a Humanist? Isaiah 14:12-17 describes the fall of Lucifer. Consider Isaiah's explanation of this fall:

> How art thou fallen from heaven, O Lucifer, son of the morning! how art thou cut down to the ground, which didst weaken the nations! *For thou hast said in thine heart, I will ascend into heaven, I will exalt my throne above the stars of God:* I will sit also upon the mount of the congregation, in the sides of the north: *I will ascend above the heights of the clouds; I will be like the most High.* Yet thou shalt be brought down to hell, to the sides of the pit. [Emphasis added][7]

With this Scripture we come to the beginning of Humanism. It began with Satan's desire to usurp the glory and power of God, to make himself god. It did not work, but Satan did not give up. He used the source of his own downfall to tempt Eve, and subsequently to tempt Adam, into the first sin of mankind. Satan has been using this approach ever since, and with a high degree of success.

Recognizing the source of Humanism helps us to understand both its appeal and its pervasive influence. Humanism is the philosophical undergirding of Satanic religion. Humanism is Satanism applied to humans. Though it may be modified from one false religion to another, Humanism is the basis of every false religion. Even the Humanists seem to realize this fact. The "Humanist Manifesto II" provides this documentation:

> Many kinds of humanism exist in the contemporary world. The varieties and emphases of naturalistic humanism include "scientific," "ethical," "democratic," "religious," and "Marxist" humanism. Free thought, atheism, agnosticism, skepticism, deism, rationalism, ethical culture, and liberal religion all claim to be heir to the humanist tradition. Humanism traces its roots from ancient China, classical Greece and Rome, through the Renaissance and the Enlightenment, to the scientific revolution of the modern world.[8]

A few years ago a publication known as the *Satanic Bible* was written by Anton LaVey, a practicing worshipper of Satan. The religion taught in that volume was essentially and presuppositionally the same as that of the "Humanist Manifesto II." The religion was Satanic and Humanistic, and serves to amplify the above statement: **Humanism is the philosophical undergirding of Satanic religion.**

THE HUMANIST MANIFESTOES

The two documents which so clearly present the religious doctrines of Humanism were written for precisely that reason: to manifest or declare the tenets of the Humanists. Christians have long followed the practice of publishing their doctrinal beliefs, but we call our works confessions, creeds, catechisms, or articles of faith. It just wouldn't seem right to speak of "The Apostles' Manifesto." Apparently the Humanists, whose antipathy for supernatural religion has already been mentioned, felt a similar repugnance in using a word to denote their tenets which had long been used in connection with Christian beliefs. So, they called their statements "manifestoes." Karl Marx had already written a manifesto, and perhaps the similarity of his views with their own prompted the Humanists to adopt his nomenclature.

The first document, "A Humanist Manifesto," (which is now dubbed as the "Humanist Manifesto I") was written in 1933 and signed by thirty-four influential Humanists of the day. John Dewey, the "father of progressive education" was, as we have noted, one of these signatories. Others include a large number of Unitarian ministers, some college professors, newspaper editors, and others. The brief introduction to their manifesto emphasizes the religious nature of the doctrines of Humanism, and the body of the document presents a philosophy of secularism.

The "Humanist Manifesto II" was written in 1973 to update the first manifesto which by then seemed "far too optimistic."[9] It is not more secular than the first, simply more blunt. It also developed some of the logical implications of Humanism which were not mentioned in the first manifesto. This document was drafted by Paul Kurtz, editor of *The Humanist,* and the preface to this manifesto was prepared by Mr. Kurtz and Mr. Edwin H. Wilson, editor emeritus of *The Humanist* and signatory of the "Humanist Manifesto I." These men are able writers, but are a far cry from the "holy men of God [who] spake as they were moved by the Holy Ghost."[10] Again, when you propound your own religion, "you can't have everything."

It is in these manifestoes that we have a presentation of the beliefs of Secular Humanism in the words of the Humanists themselves. This allows us to accurately pinpoint the cardinal doctrines of the religion of Humanism, and it permits us to carefully identify that philosophy which is presented in the Ohio Minimum Standards.

THE CARDINAL DOCTRINES OF SECULAR HUMANISM

To facilitate our comparison of the doctrines of Humanism with the doctrines of Biblical Christianity we will employ an alternating format. First the Christian doctrine will be briefly presented, and then its Humanistic counterpart compared.

Presuppositions

This is the logical starting place, for it is upon one's presuppositions that his entire philosophy of life or system of doctrine is built.

The Christian religion is built on two presuppositions. Berkhof expresses the matter in these words: "We start the study of theology with two presuppositions, namely (1) that God exists, and (2) that He has revealed Himself in His divine Word."[11] This statement is correct according to the Scriptures. Hebrews 11:6 tells us that ". . .he that cometh to God must believe that he is. . . ." Concerning the Bible we are told that "all scripture is given by inspiration of God, and is profitable for doctrine, for reproof, for correction, for instruction in righteousness. . . (II Timothy 3:16)."

The corresponding presuppositions of the Secular Humanist state that (1) there is no God, and (2) there can be, therefore, no revelation from God. The Manifesto II informs us that:

> We find insufficient evidence for belief in the existence of a supernatural; it is either meaningless or irrelevant to the question of the survival and fulfillment of the human race. As nontheists, we begin with humans not God, nature not deity.[12]

Concerning the Bible, God's revelation of Himself and His will, we are told that:

> . . .traditional dogmatic or authoritarian religions that place *revelation,* God, ritual, or creed above human needs and experience do a disservice to the human species. [Emphasis added][13]

The Humanists who have written the two manifestoes of which we are speaking are well-educated men. Their writing is clear, concise, cogent, and convincing. The world views them as learned men, wise and full of understanding. God says they are fools:

> The fool hath said in his heart, There is no God. They are corrupt, they have done abominable works, there is none that doeth good.[14]

"We find," say the Humanists, "insufficient evidence for belief in the existence of a supernatural. . . ." And God's reply is forceful:

> For the wrath of God is revealed from heaven against all ungodliness and unrighteousness of men, who hold the truth in unrighteousness;
>
> Because that which may be known of God is manifest in them; for God hath shewed it unto them.
>
> For the invisible things of him from the creation of the world are clearly seen, being understood by the things that are made, even his eternal power and Godhead; so that they are without excuse:
>
> Because that, when they knew God, they glorified him not as God, neither were thankful; but became vain in their imaginations, and their foolish heart was darkened.
>
> Professing themselves to be wise, they became fools. . . .
>
> And even as they did not like to retain God in their knowledge, God gave them over to a reprobate mind, to do those things which are not convenient. . . .[15]

This passage tells us that men who refuse to believe in God are rejecting both the evidence of the creation which surrounds them and that internal witness, conscience, which God has put within every man. As a result we read that they are 1) without excuse, and are 2) classified by God as fools.

We have seen that Christianity and Secular Humanism are opposite in their basic presuppositions. This antithesis is carried on throughout a comparative study of their systematic "theologies."

Doctrine of God

Because the Humanists do not believe in a Supernatural God, it follows that they must make substitutes. Since the Humanist does not worship God, he therefore worships man. This is done by living for himself. "Happiness and creative realization of human needs and desires, individually and in shared enjoyment, are continuous themes of humanism. We strive for the good life, here and now."[16] This is actually the worship of self. As the Christian lives to please *God* (I Thessalonians 4:1), so the Humanist lives to please *himself*. This is self-worship. Self takes the place of God.

Because the Humanist recognizes no all-knowing God as his authority in life, the Humanist becomes his own god. He becomes the final authority as to right and wrong, morality and immorality. There are no absolutes, for without a God who can specify what those absolutes should be? Each man is a law unto himself; each man is his own god. Again, this doctrine is expressed in the "Humanist Manifesto II:"

> We affirm that moral values derive their source from human experience. Ethics is *autonomous* and *situational*, needing no theological or ideological sanction. Ethics stems from human need and interest. [emphasis theirs][17]

The Humanistic doctrine of God, then, makes each man his own god. He worships himself by seeking his own pleasure, he determines right and wrong by his own fiat, he dictates morality and ethics from his own wisdom and desires. Dr. R. J. Rushdoony labels this doctrine "anarchistic Humanism."[18]

There is a second doctrine of god among the Humanists, and this doctrine we may call "totalitarian Humanism."[19] Under this doctrine of god society determines, by majority opinion, that which is best for everyone. Society, or collective man, assumes the prerogatives of deity with respect to the law. The universal laws of God may be set aside, for the new god, Society, can surely be trusted to do what is best for everybody. This concept of Society as god was a favorite theme of Humanist John Dewey, and it is also covered in the second Humanist manifesto. The Humanists call it the doctrine of "Democratic Society:"

> We are committed to an open and democratic society. We must extend participatory democracy in its true sense to the economy, the school, the family, the workplace, and voluntary associations. Decision-making must be decentralized to include widespread involvement of people at all levels — social, political, and economic. All persons should have a voice in developing the values and goals that determine their lives.[20]

Although some of this statement and other portions of the Manifesto sound facially laudatory, the practical progression of this doctrine leads straight to the Orwellian concept of "Big Brother." Big Brother, in the interest and welfare of all the people, does what is necessary to "protect" society. The concept of society as god can easily lead to "totalitarian Humanism."

But in all of this the Humanists are deluding themselves. They seek the *blessings* of a godly society in a society that rejects the true God. The self-contradiction of the Humanist manifestoes is seen at this foundational level. The Humanists suppose that they can posit God out of the picture and then go on to "strive for the good life, here and now."[21] Dr. Rushdoony, in his educational classic *Intellectual Schizophrenia*, has carefully disclosed the enormity of this self-deception:

> Whenever man asserts his independence of God, saying in effect, that, while he will deny God, he will not deny life, nor its relationships, values, or society, its science and art, he is involved in contradiction. In terms of these neglected biblical presuppositions, it is an impossibility for man to deny God and still to have law and order, justice, science, anything, apart from God. The more man and society depart from God, the more they depart from all reality, the more they are caught in the net of self-contradiction and self-frustration, the more they are involved in the will to destruction and the love of death (Prov. 8:36).[22]

Salvation

The Christian religion teaches both eternal salvation and eternal damnation, based on a man's personal relationship to the Lord Jesus Christ. Hebrews 5:9 tells us that "he became the author of eternal salvation unto all them that obey him," and Jude 7 speaks of the unsaved who suffer "the vengeance of eternal fire."

The Humanistic doctrine of salvation is quite different. According to the "Humanist Manifesto II": "Promises of immortal salvation or fear of eternal damnation are both illusory and harmful. They distract humans from present concerns, from self-actualization, and from rectifying social injustices."[23] In other words, say the Humanists, the only concern is the here-and-now existence on earth. Any salvation man is to have must be visited upon him in this life. This view of here-and-now salvation accords well with the social gospel, a doctrine long promulgated by the liberal denominations. As we have seen, the second Humanist manifesto affirms that liberal religion derives its heritage from the beliefs of Humanism. The social gospel is a good example of this fact. The Humanist doctrine of salvation is existential (only what exists *now* matters); the Christian doctrine of salvation is eternal.

World Government

A one-world government — the Word of God warns Christians against the concept. We have already considered the account in Genesis 11 in which the Lord divided the populace of Babel into different nations because it was not spiritually beneficial to have a "one world" system, even at that early date in the world's history. Daniel 2 predicts the destruction of Humanistic world government by the Lord Himself, and the book of Revelation is replete with warnings about the world domination of the antichrist.

The Humanistic doctrine of world government, by contrast, seems to lend itself to the type of one-world government against which we are warned in the book of Revelation. The second Humanist manifesto explains the doctrine of world government as follows:

> We deplore the division of humankind on nationalistic grounds. We have reached a turning point in human history where the best option is to *transcend the limits of national sovereignty* and to move toward the building of a world community in which all sectors of the human family can participate. Thus we look to the development of a system of world law and a world order based upon transnational federal government. [emphasis theirs][24]

We have surveyed the presuppositions of the religion of Humanism, as well as the doctrines of God, salvation, and world government. In examining the doctrine of God we have also discovered the Humanistic viewpoint on morality (relativism) and ethics (situational). Although the foregoing considerations do not exhaust the doctrines presented in the Humanist Manifestoes, they do represent the cardinal doctrines, and they present a background against which we may realistically view the philosophical pronouncements of the Ohio Minimum Standards.

Those readers who are familiar with the Bible will have noticed the curious way in which the religion of Humanism coincides with the Satanic world view from Genesis to Revelation. This is not to suggest that all Humanists are practicing Satanists, but it does support the words of Christ in John 8:44-47 that those who reject the Lord are "of their father the devil." They are, wittingly or unwittingly, influenced by the "god of this world."[25] Their world view, values, and mode of living is Humanistic, and Humanism is the philosophical undergirding of Satanic religion. It is, as the Humanists themselves have shown us, the basis of rationalism, agnosticism, atheism, Communism, liberal religion and other religious systems regarded as false by Bible-believing Christians. We must also remember that Humanism forms the philosophical and religious base of John Dewey's "progressive" education. Whenever the government schools teach Humanism (which they do day after day) they are promoting with the tax money of Christians a religion which violates our religious convictions. If they teach our children in their schools, the government schools are perpetrating an even more grievous violation of our freedom of religion.

We could easily spend much more time comparing the religions of Humanism and Christianity. Our next chapter, however, will provide more insight into these religions in conflict as we focus our attention on the religion of Humanism in the Ohio Minimum Standards. At this point in our study we have learned enough to realize that Humanism is a religion and that this religion is being taught in the public, or more accurately, the government schools. This is true in Ohio, and it is true across our nation today. Dr. Joseph Bean has expressed the matter in these grim words:

> . . .It should be noted here that, though most of the great philosophers supporting the creation of a world order believed in a supernatural being, one God, *humanism* is in complete control of education today. In the literature of education during the last five years, the traditional teacher with Christian faith is described as dangerous and destructive to the students. [Emphasis in the original][26]

Humanism is in complete control of education today! Is this true? In the realm of government education it is most assuredly true, and people in all walks of life, and from many parts of the country, are realizing this fact.

Does not this realization go a long way toward explaining why altogether too many young people from Christian homes and Bible-believing churches discard the church and forsake the Christian walk during their teenage years? Such young people, as they attend the government schools, are trained daily, for five, six, or more hours per *day,* in the religion of Humanism. Compare that figure with the four (or less) hours of religious instruction per *week* received by young people in the best of Fundamentalist churches, and the puzzle dissolves. We are losing our young people because they have been trained to be lost. We Christians have sent our children to the "seminaries" of the religion of Humanism. The myth of "public school neutrality" has now been dispelled; the cause of our plight is clear. For a Christian parent, the command to "train up a child in the way he should go"[27] means "do not send your child to a government school!" When Christian young people go to the government schools they are usually ill-equipped to handle the antichristian indoctrination that continually confronts them. Besides the indoctrination of the teachers and the textbooks there is also the peer pressure to conform to the group. Add to this the scorn, ridicule, and/or debasement from teachers for their attempt to take a Christian stand, and the church's teenage "dropout" problem becomes less difficult to understand.

What must the Christians do? Exactly what they have been doing in increasing numbers for the last decade: start Christian schools! Earlier in our nation's history, before we had government schools, our churches had their own schools. And the government schools were very close to Christian schools before "progressive" education made them progressively worse. It has probably been doctrinal sloth on the part of the Christians generally that prohibited us from realizing the religious implications of a government education.

The responsibility for the training, education, and rearing of children was given by the Lord — long ago — to parents and churches. Parents, for example, find careful instructions to safeguard the education and training of their children. Deuteronomy chapter 6, the book of Proverbs, Psalm 78:4-8, Colossians 2:8, Ephesians 6:4, and numerous other passages spell out the parental responsibility for rearing children. The pastor and church are also charged with the responsibility to teach sound doctrine (Ephesians 4:12-15) and to preserve the truth (I Timothy 3:15). The Christian school is a fusing of the responsibilities of the home and the church, which are the two institutions established by God for the training of children.

Governments, too, have been established by God according to Romans 13:1-7. The proper scope of governmental authority is also spelled out in this passage. The government is ordained of God to protect and encourage those who do good works, and to avenge and execute wrath upon those who do evil works. The training of children is not included within the Biblical purview of governmental power, and the First and Fourteenth Amendments to our U. S. Constitution have been interpreted by the courts of our land to protect parental rights in this vital area. Christians must "render therefore unto Caesar the things which are Caesar's,"[28] but our children are not Caesar's. They belong to God.

Summary

We have seen that "Humanism," "religious humanism," and "Secular Humanism," are all synonyms for the same religion as it is presented in the two "Humanist Manifestoes."

The history of the religion of Humanism dates all the way back to ancient times and actually antedates man. It is the same philosophy which brought about the fall of Lucifer, and its influence is pervasive today. Humanism, as we have seen, is the philosophical undergirding for all Satanic religion.

In 1933 and again in 1973 certain professing Humanists codified the basic tenets of their belief in two documents known as the Humanist Manifestoes. These publications show the religious nature of Humanism, amplify the secularism of the movement, and enable us to identify the religion of Humanism with relative ease when it appears in other publications.

We have also surveyed some of the cardinal doctrines of the Humanist religion. Covering such items as the basic presuppositions, the doctrines of God, salvation, and world government, and the source of Humanistic ethics and morality has equipped us with a suitable background to recognize Humanism when we read it elsewhere. We are now ready to examine the vital internal evidence of the Minimum Standards' philosophy in order to decide whether the State of Ohio has had, since 1970, an established state religion. For this examination we turn now to the Minimum Standards themselves.

[1]C.T. Onions (ed.), *The Shorter Oxford English Dictionary on Historical Principles* (Oxford: at the Clarendon Press, 1934), Vol. II, p. 1828.

[2]William H. Harris and Judith S. Levey (eds.), *The New Columbia Encyclopedia* (New York & London: Columbia University Press, 1975), p. 1286.

[3]T. Walter Wallbank et al., *Civilization Past and Present* (3d ed.; Glenview, Illinois: Scott, Foresman and Co., 1967), p. 270.

[4]Ibid.

[5]C.L. Barnhart et al. (eds.), *The American College Dictionary* (New York: Random House, 1964), p. 560.

[6]Genesis 3:5.

[7]Isaiah 14:12-15.

[8]Paul Kurtz and Edwin H. Wilson. "Humanist Manifesto II," *Current,* ed. Grant S. McClellan Number 156 (November 1973), 29-30.

[9]Ibid., p. 28.

[10]II Peter 1:21.

[11]L. Berkhof, *Systematic Theology* (Grand Rapids, Michigan: Wm. B. Eerdmans Publishing Co., 1941), p. 19.

[12]Kurtz and Wilson, op. cit., p. 30.

[13]Kurtz and Wilson, loc. cit.

[14]Psalm 14:1.

[15]Romans 1:18-22, 28.

[16]Kurtz and Wilson, "Humanist Manifesto II," op. cit., pp. 30, 31.

[17]Kurtz and Wilson, loc. cit.

[18]R. J. Rushdoony in an address ("Humanism Versus Christianity") at the Christian Schools of Ohio Convention, Mansfield Baptist Temple, Mansfield, Ohio, October 14, 1976.

[19]Ibid.

[20]Kurtz and Wilson, "Humanist Manifesto II," op. cit., p. 33.

[21]Ibid., p. 32.

[22]Rousas J. Rushdoony, *Intellectual Schizophrenia* (Philadelphia, Pennsylvania: The Presbyterian and Reformed Publishing Co., 1961), p. 25.

[23]Kurtz and Wilson, "Humanist Manifesto II," op. cit., p. 31.

[24]Ibid., p. 34.

[25]II Corinthians 4:4.

[26]Joseph P. Bean, *The Source of the River of Pollution* (Fullerton, California: Educator Publications, 1972), p. 10.

[27]Proverbs 22:6.

[28]Matthew 22:21.

6

Ohio's State Religion: Secular Humanism in the Ohio Minimum Standards

We come now to the final chapter in the series dealing with the establishment of a state religion. This series began on page 28. The matter before us in this chapter is of critical importance, for we will here consider and evaluate the internal evidence of the Ohio Minimum Standards to determine whether this document does, in fact, promote and espouse the religion of Secular Humanism.

As we have seen in chapter 4, the Supreme Court of Ohio expressed concern about the Humanistic philosophy espoused in the Minimum Standards within the portions "relating to the teaching of citizenship, social studies, and health."[1] Our present examination will consider the major Humanistic doctrines spelled out in these philosophical sections, and will also touch upon Humanistic tenets in some of the other philosophical sections of the Minimum Standards which the Court may have overlooked. The Citizenship philosophy (and "program") is found on page 30 and 31 of the Minimum Standards, the Social Studies philosophy (and "program") on pages 47-49, and the Health philosophy (and "program") on pages 60-62. Although each of these sections has a portion denominated "program," such portions are actually a continuation of the philosophy given in each subject. These "programs" are closely connected to their respective philosophies, they spell out the curricular components necessary for implementation of the philosophy, and they actually augment the philosophy statements, which are brief, with additional philosophical pronouncements. The "programs" cited provide the objectives which are apparently state approved, and they go even further. They deal with the educational results that the state deems appropriate.

The "philosophy" and "program" set down for each subject fit together to form a total overview of what will be taught in that subject. In other words, the State Department of Education has declared what must be taught, how it must be taught, and what should be the result. For this reason, and for the reasons cited in the previous paragraph, we have no alternative but to view this compound package as the State's educational "philosophy" for each subject that is so covered.

This is critically important, for *results* are what education is all about. The values that students adopt, the world view that they believe, and their conception of the source of knowledge are all components of the *philosophy* and the *results* of education. These components are all, by the way, religious in essence. Philosophy and results are closely interconnected. Brauner and Burns have written a book entitled *Problems in Education and Philosophy,* which was prepared specifically for public school teachers to teach them public school philosophy. These writers understand the vital link between philosophy and educational results:

> . . .philosophy and education walk hand in hand and, speaking at least of the latter, education would soon be as lost as a blind man without his seeing-eye dog if it were parted from philosophy. In this relationship philosophy and education are mutually reconstructive; they give to and take from each other, in the ebb and flow of thought and action; they are means to one another, and ends; they are process and product. It is out of the fusion of reflective thought and practical action that philosophy of education can be defined.[2]

Remembering that philosophy and results in education are integral, let us now turn our attention to the philosophy of the Minimum Standards.

To facilitate our investigation we will note some of the major Humanistic doctrines and organize under these the statements from the Minimum Standards which advocate these doctrines. We will then compare the Minimum Standards' philosophical statements with the corresponding doctrinal statements from the Humanist Manifestoes, and we will conclude each section by adducing pertinent Scriptural citations.

In surveying the Minimum Standards' philosophies we shall seek to demonstrate their Humanistic teaching in the following areas: The philosophies are 1) totally man-centered, 2) totally "now-oriented," and 3) supportive of the concept of global interdependence and a one-world government. We will also note briefly several other clearly religious topics. Let us now consider these points.

The Philosophy is Man-Centered

Wisdom and Self-sufficiency

First, the Minimum Standards' philosophy points to the wisdom and self-sufficiency of man in finding solutions to all of society's problems. This makes man self-sufficient, autonomous, and his own god. Students are taught to rely on man's wisdom rather than looking to their Creator for wisdom and guidance. This teaching supports the Humanistic doctrine of the deity of man.

The Minimum Standards say:

Problems are solved by group discussion and decision.[3] Citizenship, p. 31.

> *Man's comprehension* of the present *and his wisdom* in planning for the future *depend upon his understanding* of the events of the past and of the various forces and agencies in society that influence the present. [emphasis added] Social Studies, p. 48.
>
> Common *problems are solved through the concensus* [*sic*] *of* thinking and action of individuals in *the group.* [emphasis added] Citizenship, p. 30.

The Humanists say:

> . . .humanism offers an alternative that can serve present-day needs and guide humankind toward the future.[4] Manifesto II, p. 29.
>
> Confronted by many possible futures, we must decide which to pursue. Manifesto II, p. 29.
>
> The decades ahead call for dedicated, clear-minded men and women able to marshal the will, intelligence, and

cooperative skills for shaping a desirable future. Manifesto II, p. 29.

But we can discover no divine purpose or providence for the human species. While there is much that we do not know, *humans are responsible for what we are or will become. No deity will save us; we must save ourselves.* Manifesto II, p. 31. [Emphasis added]

The Scriptures say:

Trust in the Lord with all thine heart; and lean not unto thine own understanding. *In all thy ways acknowledge him, and he shall direct thy paths.* [Emphasis added] Proverbs 3:5, 6.

The Worship of Man

Second, the Minimum Standards' philosophy presents the pleasure and happiness of man as the ultimate and only goal of life. The practical effect of this doctrine is the worship of man, since it teaches the student to please himself rather than God. Here again the Humanistic belief in the deity of man is supported.

The Minimum Standards say:

Through all time and in all regions of the world, man has worked to meet common basic human needs and to satisfy common human desires and aspirations. Social Studies, p. 48. [Note: The satisfaction or pleasure of self is mentioned, but the pleasure of God is ignored. Working to meet basic needs is not wrong, but the motivation for such work determines the religion of the worker. If it is done solely for the satisfaction of self, the work must be seen as a worship exercise of the Humanistic religion. The Scriptures quoted below clarify this point.]

The health of the child is perhaps the greatest single factor in the development of a well-rounded personality. No individual is adequately prepared for effective living unless he has a well-functioning body and can make reasonably successful adjustments to his many problems. Health, p. 60.

A Christian would say, based upon his Scriptural convictions, that although health is important, it is far surpassed in importance by the spiritual condition of a person's heart. The *spiritual* health of the child *is* the greatest single factor in the development of, not only the personality, but the entirety of a child's life. Continuing the comparison of the Minimum Standards' quote directly above, a Christian would say that no individual is adequately prepared for effective living unless he is prepared for dying. "It is appointed unto men once to die, but after this the judgment: So Christ was once offered to bear the sins of many . . ." Hebrews 9:27, 28.

The Humanists say:

We find insufficient evidence for belief in the existence of a supernatural; it is either meaningless or *irrelevant to the question of the survival and fulfillment of the human race.* [emphasis added] Manifesto II, p. 30.

Promises of immortal salvation or fear of eternal damnation are both illusory and harmful. They *distract humans from present concerns, from self-actualization,* and *from rectifying social injustices.* [emphasis added] Manifesto II, p. 31.

As far as we know, the total personality is a function of the biological organism transacting in a social and cultural context. There is no credible evidence that life survives the death of the body. We continue to exist in our progeny and in the way that our lives have influenced others in our culture. Manifesto II, p. 31.

Human life has meaning because we create and develop our futures. *Happiness and the creative realization of human needs and desires,* individually and in shared enjoyment, *are continuous themes of humanism. We strive for the good life here and now. The goal is to pursue life's enrichment* despite debasing forces of vulgarization, commercialization, bureaucratization, and dehumanization. [emphasis added] Manifesto II, p. 32.

The Scriptures say:

And thou shalt love the Lord thy God with all thine heart, and with all thy soul, and with all thy might. And these words, which I command thee this day, shall be in thine heart: And thou shalt teach them diligently unto thy children. . . Deuteronomy 6:5-7a.

He that findeth his life shall lose it: and he that loseth his life for my sake shall find it. Matthew 10:39. [Spoken by the Lord Jesus Christ].

And thou shalt love the Lord thy God with all thy heart, and with all thy soul, and with all thy mind, and with all thy strength: this is the first commandment. Mark 12:30. [Spoken by the Lord Jesus Christ].

Whether therefore ye eat, or drink, or whatsoever ye do, do all to the glory of God. I Corinthians 10:31.

Jesus saith unto them, My meat is to do the will of him that sent me, and to finish his work. John 4:34.

Man shall not live by bread alone, but by every word that proceedeth out of the mouth of God. Matthew 4:4.

For what is a man profited, if he shall gain the whole world, and lose his own soul? or what shall a man give in exchange for his soul? Matthew 16:26.

For the things which are seen are temporal; but the things which are not seen are eternal. II Corinthians 4:18.

Furthermore then we beseech you, brethren, and exhort you by the Lord Jesus, that as ye have received of us how *ye ought to* walk and to *please God*, so ye would abound more and more. [emphasis added] I Thessalonians 4:1.

Authority for Values and Morals

Third, the Minimum Standards' philosophy features the rationalism of man for the determination of values and morals. Once again, this teaching makes man his own god, with every man doing that which is right in his own eyes (cf. Judges 17:6 and 21:25). Rather than looking to God for absolute moral law, a man need only look to himself. The only possible conclusion that can be drawn by students who are taught this doctrine is that there are no absolutes, everything in the realm of morality and ethics is relative and situational, and if rationalization can produce an excuse for any action, that action is permissible.

The corollary to this theory is that society determines what values, morals, and ethics are acceptable. Once again, this makes man his own god, or society his god. Since every man "doing his own thing" would throw society into chaos and anarchy, and the Humanists recognize this, they extend their "man is god" theology to a "society is god" theology. This permits changing values, morals, and ethics, and is in contradistinction to the absolute and unchanging law of God followed by Christians. The "man is god" theology, and the "society is god" theology are both taught in the Minimum Standards and the Humanist Manifestoes. These doctrines are manifestly Humanistic and antichristian, as we will see below. These doctrines further accept as axiomatic the innate goodness of man, which axiom is also antichristian.

The Minimum Standards say:

Common problems are solved through the concensus [*sic*] of thinking and action of individuals in the group. Citizenship, p. 30.

. . .problems are solved by group discussion and decision. Citizenship, p. 31.

In addition to teaching a body of content, the social studies are concerned with the *development of* those skills, *values,* and *attitudes that enable the individual to be a viable member of society.* Social Studies, p. 47. [Emphasis added]. [Note: The reader is reminded that *values* are a component of *religion*, as we have seen on page 32 of this work. Who will determine what values and attitudes are developed in the classroom? Will it be the parents or the church? Of course not. It will be the religious views of the state and of the teacher in a government-controlled school.]

Change is a condition of human society; societies rise and fall; *value systems improve or deteriorate;* the tempo of change varies with cultures and periods of history. [emphasis added] Social Studies, p. 48.

Social groupings of all kinds develop as a means of group cooperation in meeting individual and societal needs. Social Studies, p. 48.

The culture under which an individual is reared and the social groups to which he belongs exert great influence on his ways of perceiving, thinking, feeling, and acting. Social Studies, p. 48. [Cf. especially the first quotation listed in the next section under "The Humanists say."]

The basic substance of a society is rooted in its *values; assessing the nature of its values is the most persistent and important problem faced by human beings.* [Emphasis added] Social Studies, p. 48.

Man must make choices based on economic knowledge, scientific comparisons, analytic judgment, and *his value system* concerning how he will use the resources of the world. [Emphasis added] Social Studies, p. 48.

Organized group life of all types must act in *accordance with established rules of social relationships and a system of social controls.* [emphasis added] Social Studies, p. 48.

Democracy is based on such *beliefs* as *the integrity of man, the dignity of the individual,* equality of opportunity, *man's rationality, man's morality,* man's ability to govern himself and to *solve his problems co-operatively.* [emphasis added] Social Studies, p.49.

[Note: John Dewey is famous for his writings on *his* doctrines of democracy, the Minimum Standards speak consistently of democracy, and the Humanist Manifestoes promote a kind of democracy. The American form of government, however, is *not a democracy. It is a republic under law.* The difference is, of course, extremely significant. Remember the pledge: I pledge allegiance to the flag of the United States of America, and to the *republic* for which it stands . . . .]

The Humanists say:

Humanism recognizes that man's religious culture and civilization, as clearly depicted by anthropology and history, are the product of a gradual development due to his interaction with his natural environment and with his social heritage. The individual born into a particular culture is largely molded by that culture. Manifesto I.

Humanity, to survive, requires bold and daring measures. We need to extend the uses of the scientific method, not renounce them, to fuse reason with compassion in order *to build constructive social and moral values.* [emphasis added] Manifesto II, p. 29.

Although humans undoubtedly need economic and political goals, they also need creative values by which to live. Manifesto II, p. 31.

We affirm that moral values derive their source from human experience. Ethics is autonomous and situational, needing no theological or ideological sanction. Ethics stems from human need and interest. Manifesto II, p. 31.

We are committed to an open and democratic society. We must extend participatory democracy in its true sense to the economy, the school, the family, the workplace, and voluntary associations. Decision-making must be decentralized to include widespread involvement of people at all levels — social, political, and economic. *All persons should have a voice in developing the values* and goals *that determine their lives.* [Emphasis added] Manifesto II, p. 33.

People are more important than decalogues, rules, proscriptions, or regulations. Manifesto II, p. 33.

The Scriptures say:

If any man will do his will, he shall know of the doctrine, whether it be of God, or whether I speak of myself. [The Lord Jesus Christ] John 7:17.

He that hath my commandments, and keepeth them, he it is that loveth me: and he that loveth me shall be loved of my Father, and I will love him, and will manifest myself to him. If a man love me, he will keep my words: and my Father will love him, and we will come unto him, and make our abode with him. John 14:21, 23.

Whosoever cometh to me, and heareth my sayings, and doeth them, I will shew you to whom he is like: He is like a man which built an house, and digged deep, and laid the foundation on a rock: and when the flood arose, the stream beat vehemently upon that house, and could not shake it: for it was founded upon a rock.

But he that heareth, and doeth not, is like a man that without a foundation built an house upon the earth; against which the stream did beat vehemently, and immediately it fell; and the ruin of that house was great. Luke 6:47-49.

[Concerning the moral law of God, as presented in His eternal Word, the Holy Bible:] The law of the Lord is perfect, converting the soul: the testimony of the LORD is sure, making wise the simple. The statutes of the LORD are right, rejoicing the heart: the commandment of the LORD is pure, enlightening the eyes. The fear of the LORD is clean, enduring for ever: the judgments of the LORD are true and righteous altogether. More to be desired are they than gold, yea, than much fine gold: sweeter also than honey and the honeycomb. Moreover by them is thy servant warned: and in keeping of them there is great reward. Let the words of my mouth, and the meditation of my heart, be acceptable in thy sight, O LORD, my strength, and my redeemer. Psalm 19:7-11, 14.

[Note: When, in the King James Bible the reader comes to the word "Lord," written all in upper case letters, it simply indicates that the Hebrew scriptures there use the sacred tetragrammaton, the "ineffable name" of God. This name is sometimes rendered "Jehovah" in English.]

The foregoing comparisons have shown us clear, irrefutable evidence that the Minimum Standards' philosophy teaches the Humanistic belief in the deity of man and/or society. This philosophy is man-centered (anthropocentric), teaching that each man is his own god, with the corollary that in some areas men collectively, that is, society, perform the functions and sustain the attributes of God. We have also seen how the teaching of the Minimum Standards' philosophy, while it agrees and promotes the Humanistic tenets in this area, simultaneously contradicts the teaching of the Bible.

Let us now proceed to a second Humanist doctrine which is promoted in and by the Minimum Standards.

THE PHILOSOPHY IS "NOW-ORIENTED"

Because this doctrine overlaps, to some extent, the material covered under the second section of the "Man-centered" argument, we attempt to scrutinize it in somewhat less detail. In considering the fact that the Minimum Standards philosophy presents the pleasure and happiness of man as the ultimate goal of life, we have seen that the philosophy is "now-oriented." Let us, nevertheless, reflect on the implications of this fact.

By "now-oriented" we mean that this religion places its total emphasis on the present life, with no provision or concern for what theologians call the eternal state, or more simply, heaven or hell. The Bible teaches that men ought to concern themselves with their eternal destiny as the primary goal of life, that nothing in this life is more important. Because a man must live somewhere forever, it is only sensible that he prepare himself during this life for that eternal state.

That a Christian lives in the light of eternity does not make the present life unimportant; rather, this present life is seen as highly important because of its preparation for and determination of one's eternal state. To live in heaven *later* a man must repent of his sins and receive the Lord Jesus Christ into his life by faith *now*. He then seeks to lay up treasure in heaven by living a life which is pleasing to God. A successful life, a productive life, a life of service to others — all are desirable for the Christian as a testimony to those around him who are lost, and as loving and obedient service for his Lord.

The Humanists, because they do not believe in God, reject any belief in a life hereafter. Their belief is not scientific, as they would have us believe, for they cannot prove the absence of a future life. For this reason the Humanistic rejection of an afterlife is an article of their faith.

Since the Humanists reject on faith the idea of heaven and hell, they concentrate all their energies on the here and now, and hence the designation "now-oriented" for their philosophy. Humanism is a dismal religion, a religion with no permanent hope. Humanists are entitled to believe it if they wish, but they are not entitled to teach it in the publically-funded government schools of our state.

The Humanist Manifestoes specifically enunciate their disbelief in a life after death, and their consequent philosophy places all their concern upon the present life. Although the Minimum Standards do not specifically disavow a future life, neither do they even mention it. Their philosophy is, moreover, completely aimed at the concerns of a now-only type of existence. In this way the Minimum Standards' philosophy aids and enhances the religion of Humanism while it simultaneously and subtly attacks the Christian religion.

As we read and compare the following statements, let us notice particularly that while the Minimum Standards' philosophy says much about preparation for this life, it says nothing about the future life. Secondly, we must note the similarity between what the Minimum Standards and the Humanist Manifestoes say about *how* to live this present life.

The Minimum Standards say:

> Individuals have a responsibility of *authentic citizenship* as a member of the school, community, state, nation and *world.* [emphasis added] Citizenship, p. 30.
>
> Citizens have a responsibility for the welfare of others and for being willing to sacrifice for the common good. Citizenship, p. 30.

Religion is mentioned in the Minimum Standards' philosophy, but only once (unless we have overlooked it elsewhere). The one time it is mentioned, however, it deals with religion only as it affects the conditions of life here and now:

> People of all races, *religions,* and cultures have contributed to the cultural heritage. Modern society owes a debt to cultural innovators of other places and times [emphasis added]. Social Studies, p. 48.
>
> Man's comprehension of the *present,* and his wisdom in planning for the *future* [in this life only, no indication of the eternal state] depend upon his understanding of the events of the *past* and of the various forces and agencies in society that influence the *present.* [Emphasis added] Social Studies, p. 48.
>
> One of the factors affecting man's mode of life is his

natural environment. Weather and climate and regional differences in land forms, soils, drainage, and natural vegetation largely influence the relative density of population in the various regions of the world. Social Studies, p. 49.

Because man must use natural resources to survive, the distribution and use of these resources affect where he lives on the earth's surface and to some extent how well he lives. The level of his technology affects how he produces, exchanges, transports, and consumes his goods. Social Studies, p. 49.

The health of the child is perhaps the greatest single factor in the development of a well-rounded personality. No individual is adequately prepared for effective living unless he has a well-functioning body and can make reasonably successful adjustments to his many problems. Both are essential for facilitating learning, promoting personal efficiency, and developing successful social and family living. For these reasons health education is considered an integral part of *the total education program.* Its place in the curriculum becomes increasingly important as automation, population growth, *changing moral standards and values,* mounting pressures, and other changes in our society create new or intensify existing health problems. [emphasis added] Health, pp. 60, 61.

Preparing children and youth for this responsibility [good health] can be achieved only through a sound health instruction program organized and designed for the development of behavior conducive to good physical and mental health. Health, p. 61.

As the reader can see, the Minimum Standards' philosophy seeks to provide for the "total education program," yet not one word for the education of children about the future of their souls — not even a hint! The philosophy goes to great lengths to cover the most minute detail of a person's life — but all in the "here and now." The Humanist Manifestoes explain why this is so. As we have seen, the Minimum Standards' philosophy, like the Humanist Manifestoes, is "now-oriented." It fits in perfectly with the following.

The Humanists say:

Religion consists of those actions, purposes, and experiences which are humanly significant. Nothing human is alien to the religious. It includes labor, art, science, philosophy, love, friendship, recreation — all that is in its degree expressive of intelligently satisfying human living. The distinction between the sacred and the secular can no longer be maintained. Manifesto I, p. 44.

Religious humanism considers the complete realization of human personality to be the end of man's life and *seeks its development and fulfillment in the here and now. This is the explanation of the humanist's social passion.* [Emphasis added] Manifesto I, p. 45.

In place of the old attitudes involved in worship and prayer the humanist finds his religious emotions expressed in a heightened sense of personal life and in a cooperative effort to promote social well-being.

It follows that there will be no uniquely religious emotions and attitudes of the kind hitherto associated with belief in the supernatural. Manifesto I, p. 45.

Man will learn to face the crises of life in terms of his knowledge of their naturalness and probability. Reasonable and manly attitudes will be *fostered by education* and supported by custom. We assume that humanism will take the path of *social and mental hygiene* and discourage sentimental and unreal hopes and wishful thinking. [emphasis added] Manifesto I, p. 45.

Promises of immortal salvation or fear of eternal damnation are both illusory and harmful. *They distract humans from present concerns*, from self-actualization, and from rectifying social injustices. [emphasis added] Manifesto II, p. 31.

We strive for the good life, here and now. The goal is to pursue life's enrichment despite debasing forces of vulgarization, commercialization, bureaucratization, and dehumanization. [Emphasis added] Manifesto II, p. 32.

As in 1933, humanists still believe that traditional theism, especially faith in the prayer-hearing God, assumed to love and care for persons, to hear and understand their prayers, and to be able to do something about them, is an unproved and outmoded faith. Salvationism, based on mere affirmation, still appears as harmful, diverting people with false hopes of heaven hereafter. Reasonable minds look to other means for survival. Manifesto II, preface, p. 28.

By its emphasis on social well-being, physical well-being, mental well-being, and every other type of well-being except spiritual, the Minimum Standards' philosophy belies any claim to religious neutrality. It is totally "now-oriented," and is thereby Humanistic in this second major doctrinal area.

Against all the huffing and puffing of the Humanists the faith of the Bible stands steadfast and sure. We include at this point a brief account to remind our readers of the end of those who espouse the religion of Humanism. This account concerns the eighteenth-century French infidel, Voltaire. His beliefs would have coincided well with the Humanists of our century. Voltaire attacked the Bible publically and frequently. But when it came time to die, the efficacy of Voltaire's religion appeared in its true light.

> When Voltaire felt the stroke which he realized must terminate in death, he was overpowered with remorse. He at once sent for the priest and wanted to be "reconciled to the church." His infidel flatterers hastened to his chamber to prevent his recantation, but it was only to witness his ignominy and their own. *He cursed them to their faces* and, since his distress was increased by their presence, repeatedly and loudly exclaimed, "*Begone!* It is you that have brought me to my present condition. Leave me, I say — begone! What a wretched glory is this which you have produced for me."
>
> Hoping to allay his anguish by a written recantation, he had it prepared, signed it, and saw it witnessed. But it was all unavailing. For two months he was tortured with such an agony as led him at times to gnash his teeth in impotent rage against God and man. At other times, in plaintive accents, he would plead, "O Christ! O Lord Jesus!" Then, turning his face he would cry out, "I must die — abandoned of God and of men!"
>
> As his end drew near his condition became so frightful that his infidel associates were afraid to approach his bedside. Still they guarded the door, that others might not know how awfully an infidel was compelled to die. Even his nurse repeatedly said *that for all the wealth of Europe she would never see another infidel die.* It was a scene of horror that lies beyond all exaggeration.
>
> Such is the well-attested end of this man who had a natural sovereignty of intellect, excellent education, great wealth and much earthly honor. [Emphasis in the original][5]

The Scriptures say:

For what is your life? It is even a vapour, that appeareth for a little time, and then vanisheth away. James 4:14.

For what is a man profited, if he shall gain the whole

world, and lose his own soul? or what shall a man give in exchange for his soul? Matthew 16:26.

And as it is appointed unto men once to die, but after this the judgment: So Christ was once offered to bear the sins of many; and unto them that look for him shall he appear the second time without sin unto salvation. Hebrews 9:27, 28.

Remember now thy Creator in the days of thy youth, while the evil days come not, nor the years draw nigh, when thou shalt say, I have no pleasure in them. . . Ecclesiastes 12:1.

The Minimum Standards' philosophy is both man-centered and "now-oriented," as we have seen. It further teaches the religion of Humanism by its view of world government.

THE PHILOSOPHY SUPPORTS GLOBAL INTERDEPENDENCE

Someone may question this portion of our study by asking, "What does government have to do with religion?" The answer, for both the Christian and the Humanist, is that any government is structured on certain religious presuppositions. As Dr. R. J. Rushdoony has stated in a recent symposium:

> . . . It is necessary, therefore, that we think of the state as an establishment of religion.
>
> The state is a law structure, and every law structure is inescapably a religious establishment. All law is an expression of some form of moral order, codified and made legal by acts of state. Moral order rests on a concept of ultimate order, on a theology. The source of law in any system is the god of that system, in that law-making is an attribute of sovereignty.[6]

As this statement points out, religion can and does have a relationship to government. The Jewish and Christian religions both seem to advocate a governmental structure based on nationalism. We have previously considered the stern action taken by the Lord God in Genesis chapter eleven which destroyed the incipient one-world government at Babel and formed the basis of the multi-national world we have today. When the Lord God chose the sons of Abraham, later called Israelites, to represent Him as a testimony to His Name (Isaiah 43:10), he chose a nation, or at least, what was to become a great nation. He did not select for His witnesses a one-world government. In the book of Daniel, chapter two, we read about the image which, under God's providence, was representative of the great world empires of Babylon, Persia, Greece, and Rome. The image was destroyed by God, and the interpretation was given:

> And in the days of these kings shall the God of heaven set up a kingdom, which shall never be destroyed: and the kingdom shall not be left to other people, but it shall break in pieces and consume all these kingdoms, and it shall stand for ever.[7]

In other words, God Himself will destroy the last vestige of the world empires of men before He establishes His own rule upon the earth.

In the New Testament, we listen to the Apostle Paul as he preaches upon the Areopagus in Athens, Greece. We hear him say:

> *God* that made the world and all things therein . . . hath made of one blood all nations of men for to dwell on all the face of the earth, and *hath determined* the times before appointed, and *the bounds of their habitation; that they should seek the Lord,* if haply they might feel after him, and find him, though he be not far from every one of us. . . . [Emphasis added][8]

Paul seems to indicate that God has divided the peoples of the world, though they are "of one blood," by certain specified boundaries, for their own benefit ("that they should seek the Lord"). Apparently the peoples of the world are more inclined to seek the Lord if the world is divided by nations than if it is governed transnationally. This is borne out by the Lord's explanation in Genesis 11:6-8:

> And the LORD said, Behold, the people is one, and they have all one language; and this they begin to do: and now nothing will be restrained from them, which they have imagined to do. Go to, let us go down, and there confound their language, that they may not understand one another's speech. So the LORD scattered them abroad from thence upon the face of all the earth: and they left off to build the city.[9]

On the basis of Genesis 11, the nation of Israel, Daniel 2, and Acts 17, all of which have been cited above, as well as other scriptural passages, the Bible seems to teach that a nationalistic form of government is best for mankind. The Bible does warn us, however, that in the end times one will arise who will marshal the forces of the entire world to do battle against "the saints":

> And he opened his mouth in blasphemy against God, to blaspheme his name, and his tabernacle, and them that dwell in heaven. And it was given unto him to make war with the saints, and to overcome them: and power was given him over all kindreds, and tongues, and nations. And all that dwell upon the earth shall worship him, whose names are not written in the book of life of the Lamb slain from the foundation of the world.[10]

The Bible warns about the one-world empire of the Antichrist. The book of Revelation, in chapters 14, 17, and 18, discusses the future judgment of "Babylon the Great," often interpreted as the revived Roman empire under the leadership of the Antichrist. The Humanistic spirit of transnational government began at Babel, or Babylon, in Genesis 11, recurs throughout biblical and extra-biblical history, and culminates in "Babylon the Great." Bible-believing Christians who view the Humanistic push toward a one-world government as contributory, if not integral, to the establishment of the rule of Antichrist, strongly oppose the movement.

The Minimum Standards and the Humanist Manifestoes also have something to say about world government. The Minimum Standards' philosophy lays the groundwork for the Humanist doctrine of a transnational federal government, as we shall now see.

The Minimum Standards say:

Individuals have a responsibility of *authentic citizenship* as a member of the school, community, state, nation and *world.* [emphasis added] Citizenship, p. 30.

Citizens have a responsibility for the welfare of others and for being willing to sacrifice for the common good. Citizenship, p. 30. [Presumably an "authentic citizen" of the world would be expected to sacrifice for the benefit of the world, even if such a sacrifice worked to the detriment of his own nation.]

Through all time and *in all regions of the world,* man has worked to meet common basic human needs and to satisfy common human desires and aspirations. [emphasis added] Social Studies, p. 48.

People of all races, religions, and cultures have contributed to the cultural heritage. Modern society owes a debt to cultural innovators of other places and times. [emphasis added] Social Studies, p. 48. [Apparently this point is to prepare us for the next item on the page. It reminds us both of plurality and commonality, which we also saw in Acts 17:26. But here it is used to lead up to interdependence, which easily leads to global interdependence, which in turn is mentioned in another of the philosophical statements below.]

Interdependence is a constant factor in human relationships. The realization of self develops through contact with others. *Social groupings of all kinds develop* as a means of group co-operation in meeting individual and *societal needs.* [Emphasis added] Soc. Studies, p. 48.

Man must make choices based on economic knowledge, scientific comparisons, analytic judgment, and his value system *concerning how he will use the resources of the world.* [Emphasis added] Social Studies, p. 48.

The work of society is carried out through organized groups; group membership involves opportunities, responsibilities, and the development of leadership. Social Studies, p. 48.

Organized group life of all types must act in accordance with *established rules of social relationships* and a *system of social controls.* [Emphasis added] Social Studies, p. 48.

All nations of the modern world are part of a global interdependent system of economic, social, cultural, and political life. [Emphasis added] Social Studies, p. 48.

Democracy is based on such beliefs as the integrity of man, the dignity of the individual, equality of opportunity, man's rationality, man's morality, man's ability to govern himself and *to solve his problems co-operatively.* [Emphasis added] Social Studies, p. 49.

All human beings are of one biological species within which occur negligible variations. [Emphasis added] Social Studies, p. 49.

There we have it. Does the Minimum Standards' philosophy promote the idea of a one-world government? It would be difficult to defend a negative response to this rhetorical question. Please remember that this philosophy is required for Ohio *elementary* schools. If the children are taught this view of social studies and citizenship in the elementary grades, will there be any possibility of changing their minds by the time they reach the junior high, senior high, or college level? This philosophy of social studies does not contribute to an understanding of "the *American* heritage of democratic ideals and practices," [Citizenship, p. 30]; rather it promotes the governmental hopes and desires of one particular group of people. Which group? You can probably guess by now.

The Humanists say:

The humanists are firmly convinced that existing acquisitive and profit-motivated society has shown itself to be inadequate and that a radical change in methods, controls, and motives must be instituted. A socialized and cooperative economic order must be established to the end that the equitable distribution of the means of life be possible. The goal of humanism is a free and universal society in which people voluntarily and intelligently cooperate for the common good. Humanists demand a shared life in a shared world. Manifesto I, p. 46.

Man is at last becoming aware that he alone is responsible for the realization of the world of his dreams, that he has within himself the power for its achievement. He must set intelligence and will to the task. Manifesto I, p. 46.

Confronted by many possible futures, we must decide which to pursue. The ultimate goal should be the fulfillment of the potential for growth in each human personality — not the favored few, but for all of humankind. Only a shared world and global measures will suffice. Manifesto II, p. 29.

We affirm a set of common principles that can serve as a basis for united action — positive principles relevant to the present human condition. They are a design for a secular society on a planetary scale. Manifesto II, p. 30.

We deplore the division of humankind on nationalistic grounds. We have reached a turning point in human history where the best option is to *transcend the limits of national sovereignty* and to move toward the building of a world community in which all sectors of the human family can participate. Thus we look to the development of a system of world law and a world order based upon transnational federal government. . . . For the first time in human history, no part of humankind can be isolated from any other. Each person's future is in some way linked to all. We thus reaffirm a commitment to the building of world community, at the same recognizing that this commits us to some hard choices. [Emphasis in the original] Manifesto II, p. 34.

> The world community must engage in cooperative planning concerning the use of rapidly depleting resources. The planet earth must be considered a single *ecosystem*. . . .[Emphasis theirs] Manifesto II, p. 35.
>
> The problems of *economic growth and development* can no longer be resolved by one nation alone; they are world wide in scope. [Emphasis theirs] Manifesto II, p. 35.
>
> These are the times for men and women of good will to further the building of a peaceful and prosperous world. We urge that parochial loyalties and inflexible moral and religious ideologies be transcended. We urge recognition of the common humanity of all people. . . . At the present juncture of history, commitment to all humankind is the highest commitment of which we are capable; it transcends the narrow allegiances of church, state, party, class, or race in moving toward a wider vision of human potentiality. What more daring a goal for humankind than for each person to become, in ideal as well as practice, *a citizen of a world community*. . . . We believe that humankind has the potential intelligence, good will, and cooperative skill to implement this commitment in the decades ahead. [Emphasis added] Manifesto II, p. 36.

There we have it. A global community is the goal of the Humanist religion — a one-world, transnational, federal government. As we have seen, the philosophy of the Minimum Standards leads up to, and actually supports, the idea of global interdependence and "world citizenship." While the Minimum Standards' philosophy does not require the explicit teaching that "we should have a world order based on transnational federal government," it does support this idea by implication and every device short of overt declaration. It (the philosophy) lays out all the reasons for supporting "transnationalism" but wisely avoids a forthright pronouncement on this politically and religiously sensitive point. The practical effect, however, of teaching the component principles of "transnationalism" (global interdependence, world citizenship, and so on) to elementary school children is virtually the same as teaching the ideology of Humanism directly from the Manifestoes. The seed has been sown and the soil prepared. Time is the only requirement lacking, and with its passage will surely come the harvest of the expected fruit.

OTHER HUMANISTIC DOCTRINES

Although we will not consider thoroughly the various other

statements in the Minimum Standards' philosophy which evince its Humanistic nature, we will at least mention two of these. A detailed and careful study might be made solely on these items. First, there is the classification of drinking, smoking, drug abuse, venereal disease, and obesity as health problems, to be dealt with in health class (see page 61 of the Standards). A good case could be made for calling these problems "religious problems," or "sin problems," which should properly be considered in a religion or a Bible class. There is, also, the statement on page 49 (of the Minimum Standards) which classifies man with the "other animals." Is man, in fact, "another animal?" There are Humanistic implications in such a statement.

We will not examine these religious questions herein, nor will we raise other similar questions from the internal evidence of the Minimum Standards. The doctrinal tenets of Secular Humanism have been explained, and the philosophical teachings of the Minimum Standards have been compared to these doctrines. We feel that the question has been adequately explored and the thesis proven. The philosophy of the Ohio Minimum Standards does indeed promote and teach the religion of Secular Humanism.

Summary

In reviewing the thesis that the Minimum Standards' philosophy actually promulgates the religion of Secular Humanism, we must remember three major tenets of that religion. The philosophy of the Standards:

1. is man-centered. It promotes the doctrine of the deity of man.
2. is "now-oriented." It places all its emphasis on the present life, with no provision for the teaching of an after-life.
3. supports the tenet of transnational government. It teaches a globally interdependent political system and "authentic citizenship" in the world.

We have seen clearly that the philosophy of the Minimum Standards is Humanistic. We also remember from our considerations in chapter 4 that Humanism is a religion. Since the Minimum Standards document promotes and requires compliance with the teaching of a religion, and since this document is an official publication of the State of Ohio, we must conclude that Ohio now has an official, established, state religion. The educational bureaucracy has, it would appear, violated the United States Consitution.

ONE FURTHER CONSIDERATION

This chapter has examined the Minimum Standards' philosophy and compared it with the Humanist Manifestoes and with various passages from the Bible. We are certain that some of our careful readers, long before they reached this page, will have thought something like the following. "Perhaps CSO is correct that the philosophy of the Minimum Standards does not present a Christian, nor even a theistic philosophy of education. It does not mention God, and it is not theocentric, as a truly Christian philosophy must be. But we cannot *expect* the state to produce such a philosophy. The state, in fact, would not be allowed to publish such a philosophy of education."

Those readers entertaining such thoughts are not alone. The Ohio Supreme Court, in the *Whisner* decision, also recognized this dilemma:

> Although appellants argue that no reference is made in those standards to God or to Biblical instruction, we think it plain that to do so would constitute a violation of the establishment clause of the First Amendment.[11]

Neither Rev. Whisner, nor anyone else, has asked the State of Ohio to publish a Christian philosophy of education for us. We are, rather, insisting that the state not publish and promote a philosophy which is contrary to our religious beliefs. While we do not ask the state to establish our religion as a state religion, we must also insist that they also refrain from establishing the religion of Humanism as the state religion. And we feel that the case law available on this matter reveals that our demand is both proper and necessary.

In *Torcaso* v. *Watkins* (1961), the U.S. Supreme Court stated that, "Neither *a state* nor the Federal Government can . . . *pass laws which aid one religion,* aid all religions, *or prefer one religion over another.* [Emphasis ours]"[12] As we have seen, the Ohio Minimum Standards aid the religion of Secular Humanism by requiring it in our schools, and the Standards prefer the religion of Humanism over Christianity by ignoring a Christian philosophy of education.

In 1963 the U.S. Supreme Court further declared, in *Abingdon School District* v. *Schempp,* that:

> *The state may not establish a "religion of secularism"* in the sense of affirmatively opposing or showing hostility to religion, thus preferring those who believe in no religion over those who believe. [emphasis added][13]

Here again, the Ohio Department of Education has violated the Constitution by establishing the religion of secularism, or Secular Humanism, as the state religion of the Ohio elementary schools.

Finally, a District Court in Michigan combined the rulings of the *Torcaso* and *Schempp* cases by stating:

> Similarly, *were state* or federal *government to espouse a particular philosophy of secularism,* or secularism in general, *the establishment clause would be violated.* [Emphasis added][14]

This statement is, in light of the foregoing, self-explanatory. The state government in Ohio *has* espoused a particular philosophy of secularism, and the Establishment Clause of the First Amendment *has* been violated.

What can be done to remedy this situation? Should the state write a new philosophy of education for Ohio's schools? We think not. The state must be absolutely neutral where religion is concerned, and how can that neutral status be maintained in *any* state-ordered philosophy? If God is mentioned or incorporated into the philosophy, it becomes theistic. If God is excluded, the philosophy becomes secular, Humanistic, and/or atheistic.

But why, we wonder, does the state need to publish a philosophy of education in the first place? The enabling statutes (passed by the Ohio legislature) for the Minimum Standards make no mention of a state philosophy of education. From whence, then, has the Ohio Department of Education secured the authority to produce such a philosophy? Apparently the Department has no authority, and has simply ventured into this enterprise on its own. Is not a public censure warranted for this act?

We must insist that the Ohio Department of Education remove the philosophy sections from the Ohio Minimum Standards, and that the Department refrain from any future promulgation of philosophy. This course is, we believe, in the best interest of all citizens. For Christians, moreover, this course is requisite for the defense of that which we hold more important than life itself.

[1]*Ohio* v. *Whisner,* 47 Ohio St. 2d 181, 211 (1976).

[2]Charles J. Brauner and Hobert W. Burns, *Problems in Education and Philosophy* (Englewood Cliffs, N. J.: Prentice-Hall, Inc., 1965), p. 20.

[3]All quotations from the Minimum Standards in this chapter will be identified by the subject name under which they are listed and the page number on which they are found. All quotations are from *Minimum Standards for Ohio Elementary Schools, Revised 1970* (Columbus, Ohio: Ohio Department of Education, 1970).

[4]The format for citing quotations from the two Humanist Manifestoes used in this chapter will simply specify "Manifesto I" or "Manifesto II." The page

numbers will then be given. Manifesto I: Oliver Leslie Reiser, *Humanism and New World Ideals* (Yellow Springs, Ohio: Antioch Press, n.d.). Manifesto II: Paul Kurtz and Edwin H. Wilson, "Humanist Manifesto II," *Current*, ed. Grant S. McClellan, Number 156 (November 1973).

[5]John Myers, *Voices From the Edge of Eternity* (Old Tappan, New Jersey: Spire Books, Fleming H. Revell Co., 1968), pp. 23, 24.

[6]Rousas John Rushdoony, "The State as an Establishment of Religion" (paper read at the Notre Dame University Law School symposium, April, 1976, Notre Dame, Indiana).

[7]Daniel 2:44.

[8]Acts 17:24, 26-27.

[9]Genesis 11:6-8.

[10]Revelation 13:6-8.

[11]*Ohio* v. *Whisner*, 47 Ohio St. 2d 181, at 204 (1976).

[12]*Torcaso* v. *Watkins*, 367 U.S. 488, at 492, 493 (1961), where the Court cites favorably an opinion from *Everson* v. *Board of Education*, 330 U.S. 1 (1946).

[13]*Abington School District* v. *Schempp*, 374 U.S. 203, at 225 (1963).

[14]*Reed* v. *Van Horn*, 237 F. Supp. 48, at 54 (1965).

7

Must A Christian School, If Chartered, Comply With Ohio's State Religion?

Now that we have opened up Ohio's Trojan Horse, and have looked inside, we realize that what is there is detrimental to the interests of Bible-believing churches which operate Christian schools. We learned in chapter 3 that the Minimum Standards *per se* (that is, those requirements contained on pages 1-15), are unconstitutionally applied to church-operated schools which have "truly held" convictions against these requirements. Then we saw in chapter 6 that the philosophy of the Standards is one of Secular Humanism, an antichristian religion. We must now face the question that is asked as the title of this chapter: must a Christian school, if chartered, comply with the Secular Humanistic philosophy of the Minimum Standards?

Some people have argued that the philosophy portions of the Minimum Standards are all in the "interpretative" section, and that the philosophy is not therefore binding on Christian schools which seek state approval and chartering. This matter has been illuminated, along with many others, in the *Whisner* trial.

According to the State Department of Education

During the trial Dr. John E. Brown testified for the state. Mr. Brown, the Director of Elementary and Secondary Education in the State Department of Education, was called to the witness stand to represent the state, and in the course of his testimony he was questioned about the applicability of the interpretative section of the Minimum Standards to Pastor Whisner's private, nonpublic, non-tax supported, church-related, church-operated Christian school.

Mr. Brown was questioned by the attorney for the defense, Mr. William B. Ball, of Harrisburg, Pennsylvania. At one point the questions concerned the Level I and Level II requirements, which are interspersed among the philosophy portions of the interpretative section. The questioning proceeded as follows:

> Attorney Ball: Mr. Brown, we have been speaking here in these minimum standards, so-called level one, level two, and how do you differentiate, how does the Department differentiate between level one and level two in terms of requirement, the requirement factor?
>
> Mr. Brown: Mr. Ball, at no place within this book does it say maximal or optimum, they say minimal.
>
> Ball: Yes.
>
> Brown: Level one is a guideline for the minimal level. Those schools that are looking for quality. Attempt to have a direction moving in the level two. Here again is a guideline to a higher quality of education.
>
> Ball: Can level one be ignored by a school in terms of the Department?
>
> Brown: Should not be.
>
> Ball: Should not be. I will repeat the question. May level I be ignored by a school?
>
> Brown: No.[1]

Required to answer the question as a witness under oath, Dr. Brown stated that a school could not simply ignore a part of the "interpretative" section (in this instance, the Level I requirements). All the items listed in the Level I columns — pages and pages of them — are required for a church-related school to be in compliance, according to the Department's representative.

But the above statement deals with the Level I requirements in the interpretative section. What of the philosophy, the Secular Humanism, in the interpretative section? Perhaps a school can ignore just the philosophy portions, especially since that philosophy is a direct contradiction of the beliefs of a Christian school.

Again we refer to Dr. Brown's testimony from the *Whisner* trial. In this section also, he is answering the questions of the defense attorney, William B. Ball:

> Attorney Ball: . . . I asked you a couple of minutes ago about this provision of [standard] 401-12 [*sic,* should read 401-02], which requires a statement of philosophy, the school write a statement of philosophy.
>
> I would like to ask you this question. What if that philosophy [of the school] runs counter to the [minimum] standards? You read the statements of philosophy, and it runs in some way counter to these minimum standards orders, or it implies that a school cannot fully embrace the minimum standards, would the Department then approve the school?
>
> Brown: No.[2]

Dr. Brown answered that the State Department of Education would not grant approval to a school whose philosophy did not coincide with the Minimum Standards. No wonder then, that the Supreme Court had this to say about the matter of philosophy:

> . . .In short, *what the state gives* to a non-public school through including a requirement in the "minimum standards" that the operation of the school must be consistent with its own stated philosophy. . ., *it takes away* by compelling adherence to all the "minimum standards," *the effect of which is to obliterate the "philosophy" of the school and impose that of the state.* [Emphasis added][3]

"What the state gives. . .it takes away." This is a good quote to remember, for we will see this thought again before we conclude our study. We must also allow the final portion of the above quote to burn itself into our consciousness. With the words rearranged, this is what the Court has told us: **"Adherence to all of the minimum standards has the effect of obliterating the philosophy of the school and imposing the philosophy of the state."** That is quite a statement. It should present itself as a source of deep soul-searching on the part of the Christian schools in Ohio which are chartered by the state.

"Adherence to *all* of the minimum standards. . . ." What is required by the state to receive a charter? Let the Minimum Standards themselves remind us:

> Chartering — requires compliance with *all* minimum standards. [Emphasis ours][4]

The Ohio Supreme Court also pointed out the following:

> . . .the introduction to the Interpretative and Explanatory Information section, at page 19 of that publication, contains the following statement: "Level I details the academic and operational programs *required* [emphasis by the Court] for compliance with the adopted minimum standards." Moreover, the testimony of state witness John E. Brown disclosed that *the interpretative comments form a part of the "minimum standards,"* [emphasis ours] and that level I therein may not be ignored by a school.[5]

According to the state, then, "the interpretative comments form a part of the minimum standards." The "interpretative comments" include the philosophy statements. If this assertion of the state is correct, the interpretative section carries the same legal force as do the minimum standards *per se*. If the state is able to demand compliance with the Level I requirements, why not the philosophy sections also? The Department of Education may loosely enforce such compliance today, but what of tomorrow? Tomorrow's enforcement of the philosophy sections may be as rigid as today's enforcement of the Level I requirements — for those schools that are chartered.

According to the Court

The Ohio Supreme Court touched on this matter somewhat further, but did not, as we understand the opinion, decide the question. The Court expressed concern about the Humanistic philosophy of the interpretative section, "should that section of the publication be interpreted as part of the 'minimum standards.' "[6] They went on to say that the format of the publication, in their view, was intended to present only the first fifteen pages as the actual "minimum standards." They did not rule conclusively on the matter, however, and left the issue in question by saying, "We do not decide that issue in this case. . . ."[7]

Result

We might wish that the Supreme Court had ruled conclusively on the question under consideration. Since they did not do so, we cannot say whether the State Department of Education has the power to enforce the Minimum Standards' philosophy in Christian schools. But if they (the State Department of Education) have the authority to enforce the Level I requirements of the interpretative section, how can anyone say they do not have the authority to demand compliance with the philosophy statements that are sandwiched in between the various sections of Level I requirements? As we have seen, the State Department of Education, through its representative, has asserted its authority to enforce the interpretative section, and the philosophy passages were not excluded from that assertion.

What will be the result, if and when the State Department of Education specifically demands compliance with the Minimum Standards' philosophy, for those Christian schools under the licensure of the state? It could mean costly and protracted litigation, such as we saw in the *Whisner* case. Or it could mean capitulation. A school might decide, under the threat of charter revocation, to adopt whatever the state demands. Some men *already* take such a position, and capitulation sometimes *appears* more expedient than the agonies of an extended lawsuit.

For some Christian schools, however (and we regret to mention this alternative), neither litigation nor capitulation would be necessary. Some "Christian educators" are sufficiently overawed by the "expertise" of the state that they have already emulated as much of the state's philosophy and methodology as they can discover. Their philosophy of education is already one of Secular Humanism, and the Lord has already written "Ichabod" over their enterprise. Merely inserting the word "Christian" into the name of one's school does not make it so.

The interpretative section, including the unwanted philosophy statements, *must* be viewed by Christian educators as a continuing threat. Suggested "guidelines" may quickly become regulations when bureaucracies are involved. But there is an even more urgent reason which compels Christian schools to dispassionately repudiate the Minimum Standards' philosophy. Our attorneys have pointed out that the U.S. Supreme Court has stated the following:

> The presumption of validity which applies to legislation generally is fortified by acquiescence continued through the years.[8]

If that ruling is applied to the Minimum Standards (and to the Minimum Standards' philosophy) it would appear that the prolonged acquiescence of a state-chartered Christian school with the Department of Education could validate the enforcement of the state's Humanistic philosophy on that school. This is a very real concern, for how could a school hope to raise protectable religious convictions against a philosophy with which they have quietly coexisted for several years, especially sequent to the *Whisner* ruling?

SUMMARY AND CONCLUSIONS

We have seen that the Ohio Department of Education views the interpretative section as legally binding on Christian schools, and that the Ohio Supreme Court, while touching on this issue, did not decide it. The threat of legal coercion is therefore possible, but that is always the case when churches allow their ministries to be controlled by the state.

The Supreme Court's warning has been reviewed. Adherence to the Minimum Standards takes away the benefits of writing one's own philosophy. Such adherence "obliterates" the school's philosophy and "imposes" the state's philosophy upon the school. And this is true, according to the Supreme Court of Ohio, even without a strict enforcement of the philosophy sections of the Minimum Standards.

We may conclude from all the foregoing that the greatest threat from the Minimum Standards, whether from the first fifteen pages or from the interpretative section, is the factor of control. We must consider the issue of control in the next chapter, but we can remind ourselves of a crucial fact at this point. The philosophy of a school determines the educational result (religiously, academically, "socially," — in all areas) of the school. Adherence to the Minimum Standards, according to the Ohio Supreme Court, effectively removes from the school the control of its own philosophy. The philosophy of the state is "imposed," and the Christian school's *raison d'être,* its purpose for existence, is thereby removed. A Christian school using a state philosophy of education is not a Christian school. It is a misnamed statist school.

Does the philosophy of the Minimum Standards violate our religious convictions? Of course it does. And because it does, Christian men of character and conviction must say so. Enough of skulking about like craven cowards, bowing and scraping to the unconstitutional and unscriptural demands of the bureaucrats. The schools of CSO have taken a strong, and we believe, thoroughly scriptural stand on these issues. To our brethren we say, "Watch ye, stand fast in the faith, quit you like men, be strong."[9]

ADDENDUM TO CHAPTER 7

We must realize that the philosophy, or more pointedly, the religion, of Humanism is of concern to all Bible-believing

Christians. Whether Fundamentalist, Neo-evangelical, or otherwise, those who believe the Bible must, and generally do, recognize Humanism as the great antithesis to revealed religion. Christian Schools of Ohio is an association of avowedly Fundamentalist churches and schools. We are proud to be known by this appellation as it is defined in George Dollar's monumental work, *A History of Fundamentalism in America*, or as it has been defined by the recent congresses on Fundamentalism.[10]

Fundamentalists, however, are not the only ones to raise a standard against Secular Humanism. Some of the Neo-evangelical thinkers have also decried its dangers. Francis Schaeffer, for example, is teaming up with Billy Zeoli to produce a film warning Christians about Secular Humanism. Citation, therefore, of Neo-evangelical writers in this work is not to be construed as an endorsement of their views in other areas. Neo-evangelicalism is viewed by this writer as a Humanistic approach to certain Biblical doctrines. (Where rationalism replaces obedience, the outcome must be viewed as Humanism.) Fundamentalists, also, must face this truth. Where man's methods supplant God's methods, there Christianity yields to Humanism. Humanism favors the aggrandizement of self, flourishes on rationalism, finds a natural ally in the old nature of man. It must, therefore, be overcome by the prescription given in Romans 12:2:

> Be not conformed to this world: but be ye transformed by the renewing of your mind, that ye may prove what is that good, and acceptable, and perfect, will of God.

Christians, therefore, must evaluate every part of life in the light of God's Word. We must check and recheck every facet of our walk to determine whether we are in line with God's authority. The subtle voice of the Serpent still calls us to "be as gods."

This is one area in which some Christian schools have failed. Realizing that the philosophy of the Minimum Standards is blatantly Humanistic, we must ask this question. Why would many Christian schools in Ohio, after reading the philosophy of the Minimum Standards, nevertheless agree to submit to these Standards? Why were the Standards used from 1970 until 1974 without a great outcry from the Christians in the State of Ohio? Let us now review the comments of several Christian works that underscore a common point: our ignorance of our enemy.

Elmer Towns, in his industrious work *Have the Public Schools "Had It"?* quotes Dr. Weldon Shoftstall:

> Shoftstall noted that atheism is synonymous with humanism and commented, "Many Christians seem to feel humanism is a respectable philosophy." He noted that humanism is actually the worship of man.[11]

Christians have not all sustained the doctrinal perspicacity to identify an antichristian religion. This theme is also developed by Rev. Edmund A. Opitz in the Introduction to R. J. Rushdoony's *Intellectual Schizophrenia:*

> This book will not find favor with professional educationists, nor with those who reject the author's religion. But even many churchmen, regrettably, are more at home with sentimentality than hard, rigorous thinking. They will be uncomfortable with the way this book challenges them to re-examine things they have taken for granted. . . .Wherever government gets into the education business — whether at local or national levels — its influence will tend to secularize the schools. The churches respond to this challenge by. . .establishing — at a progressive rate — their own weekday schools. Laudable as are these efforts, it is feared that, in all too many cases, parochial and private schools operate with the same theories of education as tax supported institutions.[12]

But if the Christian schools are not based upon a Christian philosophy of education, rather than the "same theories of education as tax supported institutions," what danger is that to Christianity? Francis Schaeffer notes this danger:

> We are on the verge of the largest revolution the world has ever seen — the control and shaping of men through genetic engineering and chemical and psychological conditioning. Will people accept it? I don't think they would accept it if (1) they had not already been taught to accept the presuppositions that lead to it and (2) they were not in such despair. But many have accepted the presuppositions and they are in despair. Many of our secular schools have consistently taught these presuppositions, and *unhappily many of our Christian lower schools and colleges have taught the crucial subjects no differently than the secular schools.* [emphasis added][13]

And Schaeffer has elsewhere noted this truth:

> . . . The church has not spoken nearly what God would have it speak. It has acted as though the Christian base could be removed and it would make no practical differ-

ence to society, culture, its own young people, or what is needed to live and speak into such a world.[14]

Well then, after considering these statements as to the shortcomings of our churches and church-schools generally, can we not see that the matter of philosophy is of fundamental importance? As Dr. Joseph Bean has written, "Great cultural changes have their onset with philosophy, the area of thought where the idea is born."[15] Since the matter of philosophy is so important, should the Christians of Ohio object to and refuse to comply with the Minimum Standards' philosophy? If we do not, we have only ourselves to blame for the outcome:

> . . . We will destroy the church if we do not have the courage in a radical day like ours to hold onto the absolutes of the Word of God regardless of the cost.[16]

[1]Transcript of Testimony, pp. 53, 54, *Ohio* v. *Whisner,* 47 Ohio St. 2d 181 (1976).

[2]Ibid., pp. 42, 43.

[3]*Ohio* v. *Whisner,* 47 Ohio St. 181, at 215, 216 (1976).

[4]*Minimum Standards for Ohio Elementary Schools,* op. cit., p. 3.

[5]*Ohio* v. *Whisner,* op. cit., p. 210.

[6]Ibid., p. 211.

[7]Ibid.

[8]*Life & Casualty Insurance Company of Tennessee* v. *Ossie McCray,* 291 U.S. 566 at 572, (1933).

[9]I Corinthians 16:13.

[10]George W. Dollar, *A History of Fundamentalism in America* (Greenville, South Carolina: Bob Jones University Press, 1973), p. xv. The definition advanced there for Historic Fundamentalism: "Historic Fundamentalism is the literal exposition of all the affirmations and attitudes of the Bible and the militant exposure of all non-Biblical affirmations and attitudes."

The delegates to the World Congress of Fundamentalists in Edinburgh, Scotland (June, 1976), unanimously passed a series of resolutions. One of these was a definition of a Fundamentalist. According to the resolution:

A Fundamentalist is a born-again believer in the Lord Jesus Christ who

1. Maintains an immovable allegiance to the inerrant, infallible, and verbally inspired Bible;
2. Believes that whatever the Bible says is so;
3. Judges all things by the Bible and is judged only by the Bible;
4. Affirms the foundational truths of the historic Christian Faith:
   The doctrine of the Trinity
   The incarnation, virgin birth, substitutionary atonement, bodily resurrection, ascension into Heaven and Second Coming of the Lord Jesus Christ
   The new birth through regeneration of the Holy Spirit
   The resurrection of the saints to life eternal

The resurrection of the ungodly to final judgment and eternal death
The fellowship of the saints, who are the body of Christ;

5. Practices fidelity to that Faith and endeavors to preach it to every creature;
6. Exposes and separates from all ecclesiastical denial of that Faith, compromise with error, and apostasy from the Truth; and
7. Earnestly contends for the Faith once delivered.

Therefore, Fundamentalism is militant orthodoxy set on fire with soulwinning zeal. While Fundamentalists may differ on certain *interpretations* of Scripture, we join in unity of heart and common purpose for the defense of the Faith and the preaching of the Gospel, without compromise or division.

Unless a man holds and defends the Faith of Scripture and is concerned for the salvation of the lost, he is not a true Fundamentalist. We, therefore, repudiate and reject the term"neo-fundamentalist"as an invention of one who would discredit a movement he cannot dominate.

This definition is quoted from a special report on the Congress of Fundamentalists: Elmer L. Rumminger, "World Congress of Fundamentalists," *Faith for the Family,* IV (September/October, 1976), 9-10.

[11]Elmer L. Towns, *Have the Public Schools "Had It"? (Nashville, Tennessee: Thomas Nelson, Inc., 1974), pp. 36, 37.*

[12]Rousas J. Rushdoony, *Intellectual Schizophrenia* (Philadelphia, Pennsylvania: The Presbyterian and Reformed Publishing Company, 1961), p. xix.

[13]Francis A. Schaeffer, *Back to Freedom and Dignity* (Downers Grove, Illinois: Inter-Varsity Press, 1972), p. 44.

[14]Francis A. Schaeffer, *The Church at the End of the 20th Century* (Downers Grove, Illinois: Inter-Varsity Press, 1970), p. 30.

[15]Joseph P. Bean, *The Source of the River of Pollution* (Fullerton, California: Educator Publications, 1972), p.1.

[16]Schaffer, *Back to Freedom and Dignity,* op. cit. p.37.

8

Is the Issue Quality or Control?

Thus far in our study of the Minimum Standards, Ohio's Trojan Horse, we have examined some very potent complaints against what is on the inside of the volume. We have seen that well-respected educational experts find the contents disturbing, that the Ohio Supreme Court sees the contents as "suffocating," and that Bible-believing Christians must regard the contents as flagrantly contrary to, and violative of, their religious beliefs. Now it is time for us to tie up the loose ends of our consideration and focus our attention upon the bedrock issue that underlies Christian-school compliance with the Minimum Standards. The issue is this: does compliance with the Standards produce quality in our schools, as the educational bureaucracy claims, or does compliance with the Standards only surrender, wrongfully, the control of our Christian schools to the authority of the state?

While there *may* be some good suggestions in the Minimum Standards which could be used profitably in our church-operated schools, CSO believes that the overriding effect of Christian-school compliance with this document is state control of our schools. Because our schools are integral ministries of our churches, the more accurate reality of Christian-school compliance with the Minimum Standards is state control of our churches. The state control of our churches means an end to the freedom of religion.

To understand the reasons for CSO's stand on the matter of Christian-school compliance with the Standards, it will be necessary to reflect on several areas of educational thought in our day and to review briefly some matters of bureaucratic activity against Christian schools in Ohio. In this consideration, educational objectives coupled with bureaucratic coercion have led directly to state control of religion. Our investigation will include 1) the meaning of quality education, 2) the goal of controlling society, 3) the matter of controlling education, 4) the aim of controlling religion, and will include the scriptural view of the doctrine of separation of church and state. We turn now to the investigation prescribed.

WHAT IS A QUALITY EDUCATION?

As one would expect, the fervent affirmations of the educational bureaucrats all support the thesis that the implementation of the Minimum Standards produces quality education. We expect this sort of hopeful posturing on the part of the educational "professionals" who were responsible for framing the document. The original purpose for formulating minimum standards, as we have seen in chapter 1 of this study, was that of "requiring a general education of high quality."[1] Even if the document has not fulfilled its statutory requirement, we would expect its framers to defend the attempt. Yet after almost six and a half years under the present Minimum Standards, Ohio is reeling from the academic crisis in the schools. The bureaucrats' answer is a predictable one: we need more rigid state control.[2]

We have already noted, in the testimony of Mr. John E. Brown during the *Whisner* trial (see Chapter 7, page 81 of this work), that Mr. Brown equates the implementation of the Minimum Standards and quality of education. Dr. Brown was the Director of Elementary and Secondary Education in Ohio when the present Minimum Standards were adopted, and his name adorns the title page of the volume, page i.

Dr. Martin W. Essex, Ohio's Superintendent of Public Instruction, was at the helm of the entire State Department of Education during the time the Minimum Standards were being revised and when they were adopted, and he continues at the post as these words are written. Dr. Essex has written the

Foreword to the Minimum Standards revision of 1970. After briefly discussing the Minimum Standards, Essex concludes his remarks with reference to the hope for "improvement in. . .quality of instruction."[3] Here again, quality of education is related to the Minimum Standards. The "professional" educators of the Ohio educational bureaucracy, then, seem convinced that they have established the formula for a quality education.

Not everyone agrees. The parents, for example, who sent their children to the Tabernacle Christian School (Pastor Whisner's school) in 1973, did so to provide their children with a quality education. These parents were dissatisfied with the education of the public schools in their area. When they appeared in court, after their new school had been operating for eight months, they were very pleased with the education their children were receiving in the Tabernacle Christian School. And why not! The kids had achieved a level of academic progress during those eight months that many public schools achieve only in the daydreams of their administrators. The parents, nevertheless, were criminally prosecuted for the "failure to send [a] child to school." As we saw back in Chapter 1 of this work, a school is not legally a school in Ohio unless it is state approved. Never mind that the students in the non-school out-achieve the students in the recognized schools. The prosecutor, let us remember, repeatedly argued that such matters as academic progress were not germane to the *Whisner* trial. All that mattered was compliance with the Minimum Standards.

Many other parents are deeply concerned with the quality of education being provided in the public schools today. From the foregoing we may conclude that the shibboleth "quality education" means one thing to the educational bureaucrats and something else to many parents. In today's national controversy between professional educators and parents, there is difficulty agreeing on the meaning of a "quality education" simply because the two groups cannot even agree on the meaning of "education." The concept of "education" means one thing to professional educators and a different thing to many parents. Brauner and Burns have explained the problem in their book, which was published to teach educational philosophy to public school teachers:

> The significance of philosophy in the solution of educational problems becomes apparent *when we try to define education – such a definition largely depends upon some set of prior philosophic convictions* about nature and

> human nature, man and society. The problem, of course, is that since there is a multiplicity of philosophic viewpoints *there is no one clear, concise, agreed-upon definition of education.* [emphasis added][4]

So then, if people hold different ideas about what is meant by "education," it is no wonder there is also a difference as to what constitutes a "quality education." That which is a quality education for one man may be a horrible sham to another.

Although the "education" of bygone days used to produce high academic achievement, a high level of character development, a respect for one's country and for properly-constituted authority, and even the virtue of self-discipline, the new "education" of the educational elite aims at none of these goals and produces none. Compare, for example, this account of the high school education of Cliffton Fadiman (between 1916 and 1920) to the scholarly achievements of any high school graduate today:

> He attended an average school, with students all of whom would now be called "underprivileged," was taught a standard course which included four years of English, with rigorous drill in composition, grammar, and public speaking; four years of German; three years of history, plus a course in civics, one year of physics; one year of biology; three years of mathematics, through trigonometry. All this gave Fadiman a capacity for self-education. It also guaranteed that he would never be a member of the "lost" generation.[5]

Why not use Mr. Fadiman's education as a new set of minimum standards? That wouldn't do, for the elitist educators in the train of John Dewey don't want results like that. "Progressive" education and its subsequent mutations are the rule of thumb in today's society. Max Rafferty, the former Superintendent of Public Instruction in California, is a rarity among public school educators. He believes in traditional education, and has written numerous books in which he unmasks the deception of modern education. Dr. Rafferty has this to say about progressive education:

> Common sense told us that the schools are built and equipped and staffed largely to pass on from generation to generation the cultural heritage of the race. Every one of the other philosophies [of education] acknowledged this to one degree or another. Even in the days of the caveman it was taken for granted that each new generation was not going to have to invent the wheel all over

> again and that whatever educational process existed was set up mainly to render this utter wastefulness unnecessary. But progressive education said "No." And common sense lost.[6]

If education is no longer achieving the same results it once achieved, what is it doing with the multiple billions of dollars in tax revenues it consumes? We will not seek to list all the objectives of the new education, but will focus instead on those most closely related to the issue of control.

THE CONTROL OF SOCIETY

John Dewey was very concerned about the sociological aspects of education, and sociology was fundamental to Dewey's concept of education. He stated his belief that the "educational process has two sides — one psychological and one sociological — and that neither can be subordinated to the other, or neglected, without evil results following."[7] He further taught that

> the psychological and social sides are organically related, and that education cannot be regarded as a compromise between the two, or a superimposition of one upon the other.[8]

We will first consider the sociological objectives of Dewey's concept of education, but we will also note the impact of psychology on the education of our time. As we have seen immediately above, Dewey connected the two very closely, and this may help account for the inordinate influence of psychologists upon education today.

Dewey on Social Control

To see how education has become an instrument to control society, we need only begin with Dewey himself. In his "Pedagogic Creed" he has one article entitled "The School and Social Progress." We will now survey some of the statements made therein:

> I believe that
>
> —education is the fundamental method of social progress and reform. . . .
>
> —when society once recognizes the possibilities in this direction, and the obligations which these possibilities impose, it is impossible to conceive of the resources of time, attention, and money which will be put at the disposal of the educator. . . .

> —the art of thus giving shape to human powers and adapting them to social service is the supreme art; one calling into its service the best of artists; that no insight, sympathy, tact, executive power, is too great for such service. . . .
>
> —the teacher is engaged, not simply in the training of individuals, but in the formation of the proper social life.
>
> —every teacher should realize the dignity of his calling; that he is a social servant set apart for the maintenance of proper social order and the securing of the right social growth.
>
> —in this way the teacher is always the prophet of the true God and the usherer in of the true kingdom of God.[9]

These revealing statements might easily lead to digression at several points. We must, however, allow the reader to ponder the bulk of these teachings for himself. Let us note only two pertinent statements. First, "education is the fundamental method of *social* progress and reform" [emphasis ours]. Second, "every teacher. . .is a *social servant* set apart for the maintenance of *proper social order* and the securing of the *right social growth*" [emphasis ours].

Let us ask an important question at this point. What is the *proper* social order, and what is the *right* social growth? Dr. Dewey, as we have seen in Chapter 4, was an ardent Humanist. For him, then, the proper social order would be a society based on the deity of man and one which ignored the true God. For Dewey the "true God" was man — or collective man, society — and the "true kingdom of God" was a secular society.

But more importantly, if education is the fundamental vehicle for social "reform," and educators are to reform society according to the proper social order, who will determine what is the proper social order? The church? The home? The government? *The State Department of Education*? This concept — the reformation of society through education — obviously militates against the very idea of freedom. Whoever determines the "proper" social order to be taught in the schools is thus able to control society according to his idea of what is proper.

Dewey's pattern for the reshaping of society, moreover, is very effective. Children, in the defenseless, formative years of life, are not able to resist the "shaping" power of the one they call "Teacher."

Some of the educational bureaucrats might object to the connection of the education of today with the theories of John

Dewey. "Progressive education," some say, "went out of the schools in the fifties." Max Rafferty has answered this argument in a chapter entitled "The Fraud of the Century":

> It is certainly true that a group called the Progressive Education Association disbanded during the fifties. It is also true that many present-day practitioners of progressive education are honestly outraged when they are accused of doing what they are doing. They have been doing it so long and to such a universal paean of approbation from their colleagues that they have become convinced that they are right and the lay public is completely wrong, that they and they alone have had divine certainty unveiled to them and that anyone who has the temerity to oppose them in this matter is not only completely in error but also more than slightly stupid. To people like this, there is no such thing as progressive education because (1) that name has a bad public "image" and (2) the only kind of education there is is the one they are practicing, and it couldn't possibly be bad.[10]

Dr. R. J. Rushdoony has said the same thing in fewer words:

> . . .John Dewey is dead, but . . . it is his mind, his thinking, that's governing the schools around us.[11]

Not only is the thinking of John Dewey governing the schools around us, it also governs much of the thinking of the educational "professionals" in the educational bureaucracies of our land.

Adolf Hitler and John Dewey

Adolf Hitler, of course, realized that society could easily be "controlled" by the use of education. Hitler may or may not have studied John Dewey, but Hitler's ideas are a logical extension of Dewey's. Hitler zealously set out to "reform" society and to establish the "proper social order."

According to *der Führer,* in a speech given in 1933:

> When an opponent declares, "I will not come over to your side," I calmly say, "Your child belongs to us already. . .What are you? You will pass on. Your descendants, however, now stand in the new camp. In a short time they will know nothing else but this new community."[12]

Later, in 1937, Hitler declared:

> This new Reich will give its youth to no one, but will itself take youth and give to youth its own education and its own upbringing.[13]

These were no idle prophecies; rather, they were carefully fulfilled in the Germany of Hitler's day. It is clear that if one is not concerned with such baggage as freedom, thc control of society is readily accomplished through education.

Beyond Freedom and Dignity

Ideas are powerful weapons. One noteworthy idea about ideas is that they tend to lead men on to related but more extreme ideas. If one thinker propounds an axiom, another thinker will surely follow it with a corollary. Ideas based on fallacious and specious presuppositions easily lead to worse ideas, more radical and more devious than the originals.

That freedom is dangerous to society was postulated long ago by the Greek philosopher, Plato. The nineteenth-century philosopher Auguste Compte picked up the idea, added some thoughts of his own, and passed it on to the sociologists of our day.[14] John Dewey developed his own corollary regarding the reform or control of society through education and passed it along to the educators of our day. Some of the twentieth-century psychologists have also seized on this philosophical axiom and are exerting a strong influence upon educators to radicalize the control of society even further.

We noted above that John Dewey viewed education as having two components, the psychological and the sociological. Where Dewey's concept of the control of society is believed and practiced, educators, sociologists, and psychologists must all be scrutinized and their radical schemes blocked if freedom is to survive.

One psychologist who has exerted a telling influence upon education in recent years is B.F. Skinner. Skinner was, incidentally, a signatory of the "Humanist Manifesto II," as John Dewey was of the "Humanist Manifesto I." Skinner's 1971 publication, *Beyond Freedom and Dignity,* views freedom as obselete. In order to solve the many problems of society, Skinner argues, freedom must be replaced, and man must be controlled, through a "technology of behavior,"[15] to insure the survival of society. What good, we may ask, is the survival of society without our freedoms?

> Is life so dear, or peace so sweet, as to be purchased at the price of chains and slavery? Forbid it, Almighty God! I know not what course others may take; but as for me, give me liberty or give me death![16]

But there we go, reverting back to what Skinner calls "the literatures of freedom and dignity," which are now, as Skinner teaches, outmoded in this modern world.

It's Working

Has there ever been a time when so many people have altered or rejected the mores of their society in as brief a time as in twentieth-century America? The society of our time has been changed, has been controlled by the very vehicles we have considered, and education is the vanguard for social change. By Humanistic, godless education — transmitted through Humanistic textbooks, colleges, teachers, television, and yes, "minimum standards" — Dewey's "reformation" of American society has been achieved. We will not expand on this grim reality, but will suggest two small books for those who desire documentation showing that the control of our society is virtually an accomplished fact. First, we suggest *Public Education: The River of Pollution,* by Dr. Joseph P. Bean. Second, we also suggest *The Source of the River of Pollution,* by the same author. The publication information for these books may be found in the bibliography of this work.

According to Charles A. Reich, the control of society is complete but for one component:

> Charles Reich in his recent book *The Greening of America* says the social revolution of the new generation is so successful and complete that it lacks only the change in the political structure as its final act. In fact, our laws, institutions, and social structure are rapidly changing because of the revolution of the new generation.[17]

How did the new generation all decide simultaneously that a social revolution was necessary? The minions of Deweyism, the educators, have done their work well.

The Ohio Minimum Standards

The Minimum Standards fit the pattern of social control through education. This is true, first, because the Standards deal primarily with the external trappings of an educational motif rather than with academic achievement. They prescribe how many jump ropes and bean bags must be on hand for physical education, but mention no standard of expected proficiency in the multiplication tables, for example. They describe student services, building requirements, and staff expectations, but do not say by what stage in his education a child should be able to read. They are called educational standards, but they major on the peripheral areas of education, not on concrete academic achievement.

Second, and more importantly, the Minimum Standards present what the State apparently feels is the "proper social order." They prescribe a philosophy of education and life, which is, as we have seen, a philosophy of Secular Humanism. Dr. Erickson, whom we have quoted at length in Chapter 2, expressed this concern as follows:

> If the standards do not represent a philosophy, what do they represent? They obviously represent some view of the good life, and how the children are to be prepared for it. . . .[18]

THE CONTROL OF EDUCATION

In order to fully control society, however, the educational elitists have to see that *all* children are trained with the identical philosophy and values. The easiest way to achieve that end would be to force all children to attend the public schools, and simply pass laws that allow the educational elitists to control the public schools. This idea was tried in the State of Oregon. The State passed a law which required all school-age children to attend the public schools. A group of Catholic sisters, however, challenged that law in the courts, pursued the matter all the way to the U.S. Supreme Court, and saw the law declared unconstitutional. This case, of course, is *Pierce* v. *Society of Sisters,* 268 U.S. 510 (1925), and was decided in 1925. In this decision the Supreme Court strongly upheld the right of parents to determine the upbringing of their children and further affirmed the right of parents to send their children to parochial schools rather than the government schools.

Since 1925, therefore, state legislatures and state departments of education have known that they could not force all the children in the state to attend the government schools. Were the educational elitists stymied? Not for long. If you can't make all the children attend a state school, you simply pass a law that allows the state, through its educational bureaucracy, to *control all the education* in the state. Gary North, the Christian scholar and economist, explains the situation in these words:

> There is no education apart from conformity of thought. One thing is true and another is not. Education requires indoctrination. But the conformity of thought which is basic to all education creates conflicts when parents of differing first principles are required either to finance a hostile educational system or to send their children to it. The Puritans' solution was to enforce conformity by expelling hostile families from the community. The modern bureaucrat's solution is to force parents to finance an alternative school system as well as the gov-

> ernment system, and *then to take control of the private system later on.*[emphasis added][19]

The way to control society, as we have seen, is to control education.

How can the educational bureaucracy of a state impose its control upon the non-government schools in the state? Once the proper laws are on the books, and the bureaucracy does not "approve"—license, charter, accredit, whatever—the school, the rest is automatic. The litigation begins, often against the parents who send their children to unlicensed schools, and the attempt is made to use the courts to enforce conformity of education. The reason given to the public: We must insure a high quality of education! The State must look out for the well-being of *its* children. The educational bureaucrats, meanwhile, sit back and claim they had nothing to do with the prosecution. It is the work of the local prosecutors, they say. We did not know anything about it.

Hitler Again

Adolf Hitler was certainly concerned about controlling society through education. We have read of his plan to establish the "new community" by indoctrinating the children to fit into his concept of society. Let us now discover how Hitler enforced the control of society through the control of education.

The children of the Third Reich were all required to train in the various cadres of the Hitler Youth movement. According to William Shirer:

> To Adolf Hitler it was not so much the public schools. . .but the organizations of the Hitler Youth on which he counted to educate the youth of Germany for the ends he had in mind.[20]

All the children, boys and girls, were required to train in Hitler Youth until they were sixteen. At sixteen, of course, conscription began and the well-indoctrinated youth entered the Army or the Labor Service.

Some German parents, however, did not want their children indoctrinated by the Nazis, and sought to keep their children from entering the Hitler Youth movement. For such people, Hitler's control of education became clearly visible:

> Parents found guilty of trying to keep their children from joining the organization were subject to heavy prison sentences even though, as in some cases, they merely objected to having their daughters enter some of the services where cases of pregnancy had reached scandalous proportions.[21]

The first step to control the young people of the Third Reich was the criminal prosecution of parents. But even with this threat, some parents still refused to give their children to Hitler Youth. By the end of 1938 there were still some four million youth who "had managed to stay out of the organization, and in March 1939 the government issued a law conscripting all youth into the Hitler Youth. . . .[22] But what if the parents still refused to surrender their children? A second step of legal coercion was taken:

> Recalcitrant parents were warned that their children would be taken away from them and put into orphanages or other homes unless they enrolled.[23]

Reviewing Hitler's program for the control of education, we have learned that the first step was the criminal prosecution of parents who tried to protect their children, and the second step was to take the children away from their parents, place them in other homes, and eventually to enroll them in the Hitler Youth movement anyway. What an outrage! How thankful we ought to be that such tragic practices are not used in America!

Ohio Again

Until recently. In the State of Ohio, many parents have faced criminal prosecution for sending their children to other than "approved" or "chartered" schools. The most widely-known case is the one we have already considered, the *Whisner* trial. In that trial fifteen parents were indicted under criminal sanctions because they did not want their children in the government schools. They sent their children instead to an unapproved church school that held convictions against the state control of church schools. Many other parents, such as those in Fremont, Ohio, have faced the same charges. We do not have a documented figure on the number of parents in Ohio who have faced criminal charges for sending their children to Christian schools, but on the basis of information currently available, we estimate the number at between fifty to one hundred.

Even with the threat of criminal prosecution in Ohio, new Christian schools were still opening up. In the fall of 1975 the State brought different charges against three sets of parents sending their children to a Christian school in Canal Winchester, Ohio. Under the statute used in this case, the parents were charged with neglect of minor children (because the children attended a school not approved by the state educational bureaucracy) and were threatened with the loss of their children.

King Solomon wrote: "There is no new thing under the sun."[24] Ohio was not the first government to use criminal prosecution and the threat of taking children from parents, and Ohio has not been the last. The same procedures have been and are being tried against Christian parents in several other states as these lines are written.

The Control of Religion

We have seen that education has been used to control society, and that to do this the educators must control all of education. It is natural, therefore, that the state educationists should desire to control even the church-operated schools. But in order for the state to control our church-operated schools, it must first take or receive the authority to control or overrule the freedom of religion. The Ohio Department of Education has sought to do exactly that. Before we examine this matter directly, we must consider the nature of education and of the Christian school, and consider the realms of church and state.

The Nature of Education

Education is, by its very nature, a religious process. *All* education is religious in nature, for one cannot teach facts and train children in a philosophic vacuum. All facts are taught in a framework of philosophical, or more accurately, religious, interpretation.

In their book which seeks to instruct public school teachers in the philosophy of public education, Brauner and Burns point out that all education is built upon educational philosophy, and that every philosophy of education includes the areas of metaphysics, axiology, and epistemology.[25] Metaphysics is the theory of reality, axiology the theory of value, and epistemology the theory of knowledge. All three of these subject areas derive their content from one's presuppositions about God, about the world, and about life. These subjects are inescapably religious, and the beliefs one holds in these areas will influence his life in practical actions. The Christian, for example, derives his understanding of reality from the Scriptures, while the Humanist reasons out his own theory. The Christian understanding of values is drawn from the absolutes of God and God's revelation, while the Humanist axiology finds values to be dependent upon mankind. The Christian's source of knowledge, from whence is derived his epistemology, is God: "The fear of the LORD is the beginning of knowledge."[26] The epistemology of the Humanist is based on rationalism, on his own conception of what is true. As Brauner and Burns point out, all three of these matters, and particularly epistemology, are important to education and are found in any philosophy of education.[27] These concerns are eminently religious, and they are basic concerns of the process of education.

Brauner and Burns go on to show us that one's conception of the nature of man will have a strong effect on the way in which a child is educated:

> If a man is the special, spiritual creation of God living in His universe and enjoying earthly tenure at His pleasure, then he should be educated as such; if man is purely a biological creature, a complex nervous system lacking an inorganic mind and an immortal soul, and living in a strictly materialistic universe, then he should be educated in another way; or if man is a biosocial animal living in a given natural world through means of a received but not unalterable social order, a world in which all parts are inextricably related and of which he is an integral part, then he should be educated in yet another way.[28]

We can see by their emphasis how these authors view the nature of man, and it accords well with the typical Deweyan view. The important thing to notice, however, is that an educator's view of human nature will affect the philosophy and methodology that he or she employs in teaching. The educator's view as to the nature of man is derived directly from that educator's religious beliefs.

Education unavoidably teaches values. Values, of course, are opinions as to what is good and what is bad; the answers to these questions are inescapably religious.

Education conveys attitudes, and attitudes are based on one's world view, total philosophy of life, and other religious considerations.

Finally, education teaches the student how to live. This is to say that the values, attitudes, knowledge, world view, and theory of reality which are conveyed to the student through the educational process lead the student to a determination of how he should live his life — theoretical matters are translated into practical living.

From the philosophical outlook that undergirds every approach to education through the epistemology and axiology presented in the classroom to the final result in the life of the student, education is an inescapably religious process. John Dewey recognized this fact, and Bible-believing Christians must also recognize it in order to insure that every class and every subject taught in the Christian school is taught from a thoroughly Christian perspective. For years, however, Christians have failed to realize that the education provided in the government schools has *not* been *neutral* religiously. *Every education is religious education* in that it deals with religious questions and subjects. The religion taught in the government schools, of course, has been progressively more Humanistic and less Christian. But whether Humanistic, Christian, or some other religion, *every school teaches doctrine,* for every education is inescapably and intrinsically religious due to the nature of education and the nature of religion.

Because education is inescapably religious, it is no wonder that some thinkers have maintained the position that the government ought not to be involved in education at all. We will not argue that cause here, for we are concerned in this study about state control of church-operated schools.

The Nature of the Christian School

The church schools started by Bible-believing Christians are integral parts of their respective churches. They are established to carry out the tenets, creeds, and functions of the sponsoring churches. In short, the church-operated Christian school teaches, or should teach, exactly the same doctrine as its controlling church.

Beside the teaching of doctrine, the *purpose* of the Christian school is the same as the purpose for having a church: to give the message of salvation to the lost, and to edify believers in the Christian faith. The entire work of a thoroughly Christian school can be summed up in these two objectives.

All learning, academic or spiritual, edifies the student in his understanding of the things of God, for the distinction between things sacred and secular is a false distinction. Every subject in the Christian school is taught from a Christian perspective, just as every subject in the statist school is taught from a Humanistic perspective. The Christian school student is taught to excel in all things (see I Corinthians 14:12), including the academic, for he must "do all to the glory of God (I Corinthians 10:31)." Academic excellence is very important, and it will become part of the basic fiber of the thoroughly Christian school. Academic excellence is not, however, a feature to be offered *in addition* to a Christian philosophy of education; rather, academic excellence is a *part* of the Christian philosophy of education. Christians are to "approve things that are excellent (Philippians 1:10)," and the Apostle commands Christians to "seek that ye may excel to the edifying of the church (I Corinthians 14:12)."

Education is a religious process. The Christian school is founded to teach the religious doctrine and fulfill the religious purposes of its sponsoring church. For these and numerous other reasons, the Christian school must be construed as a part of the ministry of the local church, for *it is* a ministry of the local church.

The Control of the Christian School

Because the education of the Christian school is a ministry of the local church, such education is properly controlled, in all its internal operations, by the church. For the state to exercise control in the internal operations (which are determined by conviction) of a church-school is to take control of the church. The wall of separation between church and state is breached thereby, and freedom of religion is destroyed.

As one educational theorist has pointed out:

> Education is a rightful aspect of organized religion. The synagogues and the churches may properly assume the major task of education whenever it is committed to them by the parents, rather than to the state. . . .The Roman Church has rightly insisted by appeal to the First Amendment and the allied asseverations and documents of American freedom that it may instruct its children not as a *boon* from the state but as a *right* of the church recognized by a self-limiting state. [emphasis in the original][29]

But in order that a church retain its *right* to educate the young of the church according to the religion of that church, such church must insist on the right to control all of the internal concerns of the church and the church-operated school.

Has the Ohio Department of Education sought to control the internal affairs of church-operated schools? The Ohio Supreme Court has answered this question in the *Whisner* ruling:

> Through application of these "minimum standards" to non-public schools, *the state retains the power to regulate the following:* The content of the curriculum that is taught, the manner in which it is taught, the person or persons who teach it, the physical layout of the building in which the students are taught, the hours of instruction, and the educational policies intended to be achieved through the instruction offered. [emphasis added][30]

In other words, the state has sought to usurp control of the entirety of a church-school's educational program. What is left for the church to oversee, except perhaps the color of paint used on the walls?

After showing how the state, through the Minimum Standards, "retains the power" to interfere in the internal affairs of the church-sponsored (and other non-public) schools, the Court went on to make the statement which we have already seen, that the effect of compliance with the Minimum Standards was to "obliterate" any educational philosophy the school might propound, and to "impose" the philosophy of the state.

In considering the concerns of the *Whisner* case, the Ohio Supreme Court recognized this complaint of the defendants as valid:

> The contention is advanced by apppellants that this standard virtually provides a *blank check* to the public authorities to *control the entire operation of their school.* [emphasis added][31]

The Court responded as follows to the complaint immediately above:

> Secondly, in our view, EDb-401-02(0), which requires "all activities" of a non-public school to conform to policies adopted by the board of education, plainly violates appellants' right to the free exercise of their religion. . . . How can the state constitutionally require *all activities* of a non-public religious school, which, of necessity, must include *religious activities,* to conform to the policies of a purportedly "neutral" board? [Emphasis by the Court][32]

Finally, with regard to the matter of the control of church-operated schools, the Ohio Supreme Court specifically pointed out the necessity of maintaining the separation of church and state. The Court cited an earlier ruling of the Ohio Supreme Court which said that the best doctrine involving religion and state is the doctrine of "hands off."[33] The same citation also encourages "masterly inactivity on the part of the state, except for the purpose of keeping the conflict free, and preventing the violation of private rights or of the public peace."[34] Lastly, the Court speaks of "the necessary distinction between church and state," and warns of "the potential pitfalls awaiting unreasonable and excessive state involvement in matters touching upon convictions and conscience."[35]

Thus, the Ohio Supreme Court has upheld the doctrine of separation of church and state in the area of church-operated Christian schools. The Court has recognized that the control of the internal operation of church schools must be maintained and retained by the churches. Let us now take a brief look at the doctrine of separation of church and state as it is taught in the Bible.

Separation of Church and State: a Biblical Approach

The Bible, and especially the New Testament, teaches the separation of church and state. God, the Sovereign Ruler, has delegated specific responsibilities and limitations of government to civil governments on one hand, and to church governments on the other hand. The government of the state is one government — to which the Christian must submit, with certain limitations (see Chapter 9). The government of the church is an entirely separate government, established by God, and to which the Christian must also submit (see Hebrews 13:7; I Corinthians 6:1-5; I Peter 5:2; and other passages cited below). The Lord Jesus Christ taught that Christians must give submission both to civil government and to God's government, and that we must recognize the limitations of the government of the state. He said: "Render therefore unto Caesar the things which are Caesar's; and unto God the things that are God's (Matthew 22:21)."

The power behind the government of the church rests ultimately upon the Lord Jesus Christ, who is the Head of the Church: "And [the Father] hath put all things under his feet, and gave him to be the head over all things to the church. . . .(Ephesians 1:22)." See also Colossians 1:18. There are some differences in church polity (government) from church to church, but all Bible-believing churches confess Christ as the Head, the Lord of the church. He exercises His leadership through the Scriptures and by the Holy Spirit's leading in the men duly ordained to serve as the leaders of the church. We will not launch into a discussion on church polity, for it is a large area of study, but we will list several passages of Scripture that deal with the government of the church and show it to be separate from the government of the state: Acts 15; Ephesians 4:11-16; I Timothy 3; Titus 1; I Peter 5:1-4; and Acts 20:28-32. The Scriptures cited give us the qualifications for those who lead the church and explain the responsibilities these men must exercise under the Lordship of Christ.

The New Testament also contains several passages which show the responsibilities of civil government, such as Romans 13:1-7; I Timothy 2:1-4; and I Peter 2:13-17. These passages will be examined in Chapter 9, so we will not deal with them here.

A study of the passages mentioned above reveals that the Scriptures teach a separation of church and state. The government of church and the government of state are always presented separately, and if each is governed properly their responsibilities complement one another but do not overlap.

The several states of the United States and also the federal government have assumed a great amount of responsibility in the education of children, but that does not mean they are justified in retaining this responsibility. As we have seen, education is inescapably religious and doctrinal in content. To determine whether church or state has the primary responsibility for the control of education offered in the church, we must ask the question, "Which government is responsible for the teaching of doctrine?" The answer, of course, is that the church, through the pastor, is responsible for teaching doctrine. The pastor is the undershepherd to the Lord Jesus Christ, and is charged with teaching sound doctrine:

> And he gave some. . .pastors and teachers;
>
> For the perfecting of the saints, for the work of the ministry, for the edifying of the body of Christ:
>
> Till we all come in the unity of the faith, and of the knowledge of the Son of God, unto a perfect man, unto the measure of the stature of the fulness of Christ:
>
> That we henceforth be no more children, tossed to and fro, and carried about with every wind of doctrine, by the sleight of men, and cunning craftiness, whereby they lie in wait to deceive;
>
> But speaking the truth in love, may grow up into him in all things, which is the head, even Christ:
>
> From whom the whole body fitly joined together and compacted by that which every joint supplieth, according to the effectual working in the measure of every part, maketh increase of the body unto the edifying of itself in love.[36]

This passage is a description of the work of the pastor-teacher. It shows his responsibility under Christ to teach sound doctrine to the church, and its teaching is augmented in I Timothy 4:14-16 and 5:17 as well as in Titus 2:1. This passage is also a perfect description of the ministry of the Christian school, for the Christian school is an integral part of the church. One of the great blessings of the Christian school is the fact that where children are carefully taught sound doctrine they will grow up without being "tossed to and fro, and carried about with every wind of doctrine. . . ."

Let us note two further thoughts from Ephesians 4:11. First, the apostles and prophets were given to the church in its incipient years, but these positions are no longer exercised by current leaders. The apostles of the church laid the foundation for the church in all ages, and "hence they are the apostles of the Church in the present day as well as they were the apostles of the primitive Church."[37] The special gift of a prophet was temporary in nature.[38] Evangelists still perform their ministries today, but are not responsible for the day to day teaching in a given church, as is the pastor.

Second, the structure of the Greek in Ephesians 4:11, both in the Textus Receptus and the critical editions, shows clearly that the phrase "pastors and teachers" refers to a single office, that of the pastor-teacher. The pastor, or shepherd, is also the chief teacher of the local church. In this way every pastor is called to be an educator.

If the state is given control of the Christian school, which is a part of the church, then the Lordship of Christ has been replaced by the lordship of the state. In this situation the state becomes the head of the church. This situation is both unscriptural and contrary to the well-established "separation of church and state" doctrine which has been respected since the inception of our republic. We do not allow the state to charter our Sunday Schools, choose our pastors, or formulate minimum standards for our prayer meetings. Similarly, we must not surrender to the state the authority to control our Christian schools.

For the Good of the State

The usual reason proffered by state officials for their interference in the Christian schools is that the state must control education to protect itself, or to promote the good of the state. This reason is also couched in language such as "for the protection of the child," "to insure a quality education," and other similar maxims. All these benign-sounding phrases mean essentially the same thing, however, that the state must control the church for the good of society. Professor Patrick Halpin has shown that this argument is an ancient and oft-repeated phrase in the repertory of state officials seeking to control religion:

> It is to be noted that whenever the state pressed heavily against the church, the reason put forward was the weal of the state. This has always been the war cry.[39]

And this has been the war cry of the Ohio bureaucrats in their attempt to control Christian education in this state. It is echoed in the state capitols of our land and in the hallways of Washington. Christian citizens of our day must be prepared to counter this argument if freedom of education is to be preserved in our nation.

Controlling Religion in Ohio

If education is to control society, as we have seen, then all education in the state must be controlled by the state. The church-operated Christian schools, when prosecuted, seek for refuge under the freedom of religion guarantees of the First Amendment. The case of Pastor Whisner and his co-defendants is an example of this defense.

The educational bureaucrats in Ohio, not wanting to lose their control over the Christian schools, sought to overrule the religious freedom protections in the Constitution. We have already mentioned the *amicus curiae* brief submitted by Dr. Martin W. Essex, the Ohio Superintendent of Public Instruction, against Rev. Levi Whisner and his co-defendants. Let us refresh our memories as to the wording of that brief, that we may see how Superintendent Essex' legal propositions, had the Supreme Court accepted them, would have taken from the Tabernacle Christian School, and from all the Christian schools in Ohio, the ability to protect the church control of these schools as a matter of religious liberty. The Essex brief argues that:

> If defendants have presented evidence sufficient to support a claim of religious infringement by the State through its Minimum Standards, must the religious freedom necessarily prevail? Clearly not.[40]

Then follows a discussion of the reasons why the freedom of religion should be denied the defendants. We will not examine these reasons here, since the Court did not accept them as valid. We regard the end result of Essex' reasoning as the most important consideration of this brief. In the concluding statements of the brief, the proposition to deny Pastor Whisner and the others their religious liberty is again propounded:

> Even if defendants were to have stated a claim for relief under the Free Exercise Clause, the State's interests in providing for a compulsory minimum standard of education clearly outweighs whatever minor infringement on defendants' religious practices may result.[41]

We may hope that all Christians understand the implications of this proposition. If Dr. Essex had had his way, the State of Ohio would have given the educators the authority to control our Christian schools, a power which also includes the control of religion by the state. By the grace of God, however, the Ohio Supreme Court ruled strongly against this proposition.

Not everyone has understood that the Ohio Department of Education intends to control our Christian schools, but even the Cleveland *Plain Dealer* recognized that the matter of bureaucratic control was involved. Said this newspaper in an editorial on July 30, 1976:

> Martin W. Essex, superintendent of education, whose power and bureaucratic domain have been diminished by this decision, reacted predictably. He suggested the court was establishing the "right of ignorance" and promoting "white flight" to avoid the integrated public schools. He missed the point.[42]

That Essex reacted predictably we may agree. That he missed the point we dispute. As we see the matter, and taking into consideration the clear intentions of Essex' brief, he understood the point fully. He may have raised the non-related issues as an evasive screen for the benefit of the newspapers and their readers, but he undoubtedly realized that his power had been curtailed by the Supreme Court's ruling. His other comments, in fact, show that he intends to re-establish his, and the state's, control over the church-operated schools. The *Plain Dealer* of July 29 quotes him as saying:

> Apparently, it [the *Whisner* decision] will neccessitate [*sic*] or require a separate set of standards for religious schools in Ohio. I would urge the State Board of Education to act promptly.[43]

The immediate reaction of Superintendent Essex, when one set of Standards was declared unconstitutional, was to ask for another set. The state must, after all, control all education in the state. It must control all the religious schools in the state. It must protect the welfare of its children.

The end of this matter has not yet been reached. The state educational bureaucracy will doubtless promulgate a new set of standards to control the education of church-operated schools. It may bring more lawsuits to our schools, but we know what is right. The Scriptures show us the proper policy, and the Ohio Supreme Court has also told us. The best policy is "hands off." To that we say, "Amen."

What About Future Regulations?

As everyone knows, it is the nature of bureaucracies to increase regulations, not to diminish them. A recent article in the Cleveland *Plain Dealer,* for example, dealt with the problem of the lack of quality in the public schools of Ohio. So many Ohio citizens are complaining about the schools, and have voiced their complaints to their legislators, that now the legislators are concerned. Many people are pushing for "back to basics" education in the public schools. The teachers' union, of course, opposes "back to basics" education. The bureaucrats, at least bureaucrat Essex, sees the answer in greater state control of education. Said Essex (as quoted by The *Plain Dealer*):

> We're moving in the most radical redesign of education in Ohio of anywhere in the nation. We're in the process of restructuring all 51 teacher education institutions in Ohio.
>
> As a response to citizen displeasure, he said, "One of the requirements of this redesign of teacher education is that each teacher, whether it be the teacher of physics or art or industrial arts or English, that that teacher shall have the capability of teaching reading before the person can receive a license to teach."[44]

A license to teach? That indicates that more state control of education is on the way, for there is currently no teacher licensing program in Ohio. If the public schools would just teach the students to read in kindergarten, as the Christian schools do, they wouldn't need to teach all their teachers how to teach reading. Besides, how can the teachers cover their subject matter properly if they have to waste time teaching reading, which should have been learned in kindergarten?

Licensing teachers can be a dangerous concern to Christian schools, as Christian educators in Michigan well know. It is possible to institute a procedure for licensing teachers that discriminates against Christian teachers in one way or another.

The point is, of course, that the bureaucrats mean to increase their control, not see it diminished. It is no matter to them that increased state control of education has hurt education.

The attorneys for Christian Schools of Ohio (CSO) have warned us about a number of serious legal implications related to state control of Christian schools. The following does not constitute legal advice. It is merely a report of what CSO's legal counsellors have informed us, their clients. Before a school takes *any* steps with regard to the Minimum Standards, CSO recommends consultation with a competent Christian attorney who is well-versed in both school and constitutional law. We know that such lawyers are sometimes difficult to locate. Should any Christian schools have need of such a lawyer they may call the CSO office in Cleveland, Ohio, and we will be happy to recommend one.

The difference between preference and conviction. Based on the U.S. Supreme Court decision in *Wisconsin* v. *Yoder* the courts differentiate between beliefs which are "preferences" and beliefs which are "convictions." Preferences are not protectable under the First Amendment, but convictions are. Preferences are beliefs that a man will change under some circumstances. Convictions, however, are beliefs that a man will never change, regardless of the consequences.

How the courts determine when convictions are truly held. The courts have the authority to determine whether a man's convictions are "truly held." The Ohio Supreme Court, for example, ruled in *Whisner* that the religious convictions of the defendants against accepting a state charter for their school were truly held. The courts determine whether convictions are truly held by looking at the life of the person claiming the conviction. If there is a truly-held conviction, say the courts, it will manifest itself in the actions of the person or other entity in question.

This concept is sound, not only legally, but also scripturally. James 2:17 and 18, for example, teach us that:

> . . .faith, if it hath not works, is dead, being alone. Yea, a man may say, Thou hast faith, and I have works: shew me thy faith without thy works, and I will shew thee my faith by my works.

James, in other words, says that if a man has faith, the results of it will be seen in his life.

Let us apply this test to the Minimum Standards. If this document violates a school's religious convictions, the courts expect that the school will have notified the state that such is the case. According to our attorneys this convictional stand must be made before litigation is begun against the school. It should be made as soon as the governing body of the school and/or of the church recognizes that the Standards violate their convictions. Our attorneys have further advised us that if a Christian school *does* have religious convictions against the Minimum Standards, *now* is the time to say so, if they have not done so already. If the school does not object to the standards now, and it simply remains quiet about its convictions, the courts would be unlikely to recognize any future claim to convictions against the Standards as valid or "truly held."

Future regulations. If Christian schools do not object to the control of their schools by the state *now,* after the *Whisner* ruling, how can they raise such a conviction later on? When the state publishes the new, more restrictive standards, the Christian school that remains silent now may not be able to sustain a defense based on religious convictions. The courts may not recognize as "truly held" a conviction against the state control of a church-operated Christian school in the future if that school has no problem with the state control of that same school now. **The degree of control is immaterial once the principle of control has been accepted.**

The doctrine of ratification. Furthermore, our attorneys say, there is a legal doctrine known as ratification. When a far-reaching decision, such as *Whisner,* is made by the courts, and similarly-situated parties do nothing to change their relationship to the laws, these parties, in effect, ratify the laws. They make the laws binding on themselves by their acquiescence. Our lawyers have pointed out this ruling of the U.S. Supreme Court, made in 1933:

> The presumption of validity which applies to legislation generally is fortified by acquiescence continued through the years.[45]

According to this ruling, a Christian school that continues to acquiesce to the Minimum Standards thereby validates those standards as to that school.

Furthermore, our attorneys warn us, there is not an official length of time when the doctrine of ratification takes effect. They warn us that, on the basis of other decisions of the courts, six months might be a reasonable length of time to allow before the courts would consider the law ratified. The *Whisner* decision was handed down on July 28, 1976.

Approval is easier to get now. We have heard reports that indicate it is now easier than ever before for a new Christian school in Ohio to receive both state approval and a state charter. This condition should alert Christians that something is awry. Every school that accepts state licensure today may be forfeiting its ability to resist state control tomorrow. Once all the cows are in the barn, the farmer slams the door and locks it. Then the animals cannot get out.

Summary and Conclusion

What is the issue at the heart of the controversy concerning the state regulation of Christian schools? Must the state license church schools for the protection and the well-being of society, and to insure that each child receives a quality education? No, the state must not be allowed to control our church-operated Christian schools. They are integral ministries of our churches. State control of a church-operated Christian school is state control of its supporting church.

The state may prescribe what is a quality education for the government (public) schools, but not what is a quality education for the church schools, because there is no absolute definition of education. One's definition of education is determined by his philosophical presuppositions. The Ohio Department of Education has ignored academic achievement and bases its assumptions of quality solely on the matter of compliance with the bureaucratic regulations. This assumption is, as we have seen many times over, gratuitous. It is simply unsupported by fact.

Professional educators have endorsed control of society through education, and they have sought to control all of education to implement their goal. They have even sought to control religion in their grasp for power. The Ohio Supreme Court has endorsed a policy of governmental "hands off" for our church-operated schools. Christian schools which ignore this advice may be forfeiting the opportunity to claim religious convictions against the future state control of their educational program.

State control of Christian schools cannot insure the kind of quality that a Christian school demands. Not adherence to the state's Minimum Standards, but adherence to God's Maximum Standards, given us in the Word of God, will insure quality in the Christian school. There is only one thing state control insures for Christian schools. That is more state control.

[1]Ohio Revised Code, Sec. 3301.07.

[2]The [Cleveland] *Plain Dealer,* November 27, 1976, p. 10-A.

[3]*Minimum Standards for Ohio Elementary Schools,* op. cit., p. iii.

[4]Charles J. Brauner and Hobert W. Burns, *Problems in Education and Philosophy* (Englewood Cliffs, New Jersey: Prentice-Hall, Inc., 1965), p. 15.

[5]Rousas J. Rushdoony, *Intellectual Schizophrenia* (Philadelphia, Pennsylvania: The Presbyterian and Reformed Publishing Company, 1961), p. 35.

[6]Max Rafferty, *What They Are Doing to Your Children* (New York: The New American Library of World Literature, Inc., 1963, 1964), p. 63.

[7]John Dewey, "My Pedagogic Creed," *John Dewey on Education: Selected Writings,* ed. Reginald D. Archambault (New York: Random House, Inc., 1964), p. 428.

[8]Ibid., pp. 428, 429.

[9]Ibid., pp. 438, 439.

[10]Rafferty, op. cit., pp. 67, 68.

[11]Dr. Rousas J. Rushdoony in an address ("Religious Goals of Humanism") at the Christian Schools of Ohio Convention, Mansfield Baptist Temple, Mansfield, Ohio, October 15, 1976.

[12]William L. Shirer, *The Rise and Fall of the Third Reich* (New York: Simon and Schuster, Inc., 1960), p. 249.

[13]Ibid.

[14]Erica Carle, *The Hate Factory* (Milwaukee, Wisconsin: The Erica Carle Foundation, 1974), pp. 11-13.

[15]B. F. Skinner, *Beyond Freedom and Dignity* (New York: Bantam Books, Inc., 1971), pp. 1-23.

[16]Patrick Henry, "Speech in the Virginia Convention," *Adventures in American Literature* ed. John Gehlmann et al., (New York: Harcourt, Brace & World, Inc., 1958), p. 472.

[17]Joseph P. Bean, *Public Education River of Pollution* (Fullerton, California: Educator Publications, n. d.), p. 4.

[18]Transcript of Testimony, p. 263, *Ohio* v. *Whisner*, 47 Ohio St. 2d 181 (1976).

[19]Gary North, "Educational Vouchers: The Double Tax," *The Freeman*, XXVI, (May, 1976), 260.

[20]Shirer, op. cit., p. 252.

[21]Ibid., p. 253.

[22]Ibid., p. 255.

[23]Ibid.

[24]Ecclesiastes 1:9.

[25]Brauner and Burns, op. cit., p. 7.

[26]Proverbs 1:7.

[27]Brauner and Burns, op. cit., pp. 4-15.

[28]Ibid., p. 18.

[29]George Huntston Williams, "Church-State Separation and Religion in the Schools of Our Democracy," *Selected Readings in the Philosophy of Education*, ed., Joe Park (New York: The Macmillan Co., 1963), p. 513.

[30]*Ohio* v. *Whisner*, 47 Ohio St. 2d 181, at 215 (1976).

[31]Ibid., p. 201.

[32]Ibid., p. 207.

[33]Ibid., p. 206.

[34]Ibid., pp. 208, 209.

[35]Ibid., p. 209.

[36]Ephesians 4:11-16.

[37]L. Berkhof, *Systematic Theology* (Grand Rapids, Michigan: Wm. B. Eerdmans Publishing Co., 1941), p. 585.

[38]Ibid.

[39]Patrick A. Halpin, "Church and State," *Encyclopedia Americana* (1954), VI, 655.

[40]Brief of *amicus curiae* for the Superintendent of Public Instruction, *Ohio* v. *Whisner*, 47 Ohio St. 2d 181 (1976), p. 12.

[41]Ibid., p. 20.

[42]Editorial, "A Basic Right Upheld," *The* [Cleveland] *Plain Dealer*, July 30, 1976, p. 6-B.

[43]George E. Condon, Jr., "State Hold on Church Schools Upset," The *Plain Dealer*, July 29, 1976, p. 14-A.

[44]George E. Condon, Jr., "Interest In School Quality Increases in Legislature," The *Plain Dealer*, November 27, 1976, p. 10-A.

[45]*Life & Casualty Insurance Company of Tennessee* v. *Ossie McCray*, 291 U.S. 566 at 572, (1933).

9

To Be, Or Not To Be (Chartered) — That Is The Question

When in the course of human events, it becomes necessary for Christian people, who are God-fearing and law-abiding citizens, to refuse to comply with the bureaucratic regulations promulgated by the State Board of Education, and to maintain the doctrine known as "separation of church and state," which the laws of our land have established, and which accords with the church polity taught in the Christian Scriptures, a decent respect to the opinions of all concerned requires that they should declare the causes which impel them to the maintenance of this separation.

The major causes that have led Christians to refuse the state chartering and state control of their church-operated Christian schools have already been presented in the previous chapters of this work. They have been carefully documented and, we hope, carefully explained. We will now consider some of the reasons that have been adduced *in favor* of chartering Christian schools, especially here in the State of Ohio. These arguments will then be rebutted, and a summary of the reasons which militate against the state control of church schools will be presented.

Two Associations

At this point we will mention something that most Christian educators in Ohio already know, but which may not be known to some people in other states. There are, in Ohio, two Christian school associations composed of Bible-believing Christian schools and churches. This study represents the position of Christian Schools of Ohio, known to most people as CSO. The other association is the Ohio Association of Christian Schools, or OACS. We should point out that the OACS has no affiliation with the AACS, the American Association of Christian Schools, whereas CSO has been associated with the AACS and has much in common with the position of AACS.

The Ohio Association of Christian Schools, through their spokesmen, and in contrast to CSO, has strongly supported the position of the state chartering of Christian schools. The OACS has maintained this position steadfastly throughout the *Whisner* case and the *Canal Winchester* case. Even after the *Whisner* ruling was delivered by the Ohio Supreme Court, the OACS position as to the state chartering of Christian schools has not changed.

The CSO position, on the other hand, has been modified as it has grown stronger and more consistent with the Scriptures and the historical Christian stand. Prior to the *Whisner* decision CSO had six chartered schools and a majority of unchartered schools. Each school then made its own decision as to whether to seek a state charter. As this chapter is being written, those schools of CSO which have received charters are taking steps to divest themselves of the state charters.

Even though some member schools of CSO had obtained state charters, CSO has consistently spoken against the current Minimum Standards. Through careful study of the Scriptures, the Constitution and laws of our land, the Minimum Standards, the nature of education, the implications of the state control of church-operated schools, and the responsibility of parents and churches to impart correct doctrine to their young, the leaders and members of CSO have arrived at a position which we believe is fully consistent with the Scriptures, our Christian presuppositions, and the U.S. Constitution. The CSO position is this: state control of church education is wrong. It is certainly wrong under the present Minimum Standards, as this entire study has shown, and it is also wrong under any "minimum" standards that interfere with the internal operation of a church's ministry. The education given in our church-operated Christian schools is scriptural education, based on a Christian world view, a Christian epistemology, Christian values, Christian metaphysics, and Christian doctrine. All the subjects in the curriculum have a Christian perspective; there are no "secular" subjects in a truly Christian school. The methodology, curriculum, philosophy, objectives, organization, administration, staff, teachers, instructional materials, and all other internal facets of education are determined by the church, and are not, therefore, within the proper control or purview of the state. When parents take their children out of the state schools they are expressing, in varying degrees, a dissatisfaction with the instruction received in those schools. When they place their children in a Christian school they are entrusting the education of their child *to the church* which operates that school and they are removing, thereby, the responsibility of education *from the state*.

This positional conviction was fortified and vindicated by the *Whisner* opinion of the Ohio Supreme Court in July, 1976.

If the members of CSO are criticized for not seeing this position in its full consistency before, so be it. Insufficient light sometimes makes the truth difficult to see. Our members have acted in good faith; they have done that which seemed right and proper at the time; as their understanding and insight of this matter has matured they have taken and are taking steps to operate their Christian schools in line with a fully consistent scriptural position which they have more clearly seen after deeper reflection and study.

Reasons Supporting Compliance

To take a stand in favor of the state licensure (chartering) of Christian schools, the OACS has put forward several reasons supporting their position. We have seen no systematic positional statement from the OACS, but their stand has been taken publically, and their reasons have been given wide exposure. To collect the various arguments in favor of Christian school licensure by the state we in CSO have talked to some members of the OACS, we have had limited correspondence with some, we have read everything that has come to our attention concerning this matter, both from the OACS office and from its member schools. We have also read and studied the public statements of OACS which have appeared in newspapers and other periodicals.

Because it is normal for the spokesmen of any group to present their strongest arguments in situations such as those mentioned above, and because such spokesmen would naturally desire to express their most cogent and persuasive reasons for their actions, we are assuming that we have read or heard the best reasons OACS has for recommending compliance with the Ohio Minimum Standards and the attendant state control of their Christian schools.

In the absence of a systematic positional statement by the OACS we will consider the several arguments in favor of Christian school compliance to which we have been exposed from the writings of the OACS. In addition we will consider three other questions about this matter which we have not seen as arguments from the OACS, but which are on people's minds. We have taken care to present the OACS arguments accurately, so that we do not misrepresent their position. Here then are the reasons cited *in support* of Christian school compliance with the Ohio Minimum Standards and the state licensure of Christian schools.

1. A Positive Image

The Ohio Education Association, or OEA, is the public school teachers' union in Ohio. The OEA publishes a monthly magazine entitled *Ohio Schools.* Lou E. Koloze, the Executive Director of the OACS, was quoted in an interview given to *Ohio Schools* as saying:

> "We believe in working in a systematic internal way to give Christian schools a positive image," he told *Ohio Schools.* "I think our brothers on the other side (CSO) think more in terms of working with the legislature in a more open type of activity than we would believe in."
>
> He explained that his organization works with the State Department of Education and requires its members either to be accredited by the State Board or to have accreditation as their goal.
>
> That differs greatly from the total government hands off attitude taken by CSO.[1]

It should be noted that members of CSO *do* sometimes talk to our elected representatives in the legislature or the State Board of Education. This is participation in representative government, and we are not sure what the objection to this practice might be, but we proceed to the central issue. Koloze has said that the OACS schools are working toward a "positive image," and this procedure includes seeking state charters. Mr. Koloze did not state for whom this positive image is being sought. Is it for parents, the community, or the State Department of Education?

A "positive image" sounds like a nice goal, but if it means surrendering the control of the school, and more accurately, the control of the church to the government, then it surely falls into the category of selling one's birthright for a bowl of sodden pottage. Esau got his pottage all right, but he lived to regret the loss of his birthright.

Christians cannot always do that which produces a "positive image" in the eyes of the world, and neither is that the purpose of our sojourn. Often our stand will cause the reproach of the world, as we are taught in the Word:

> Wherefore Jesus also, that he might sanctify the people with his own blood, suffered without the gate. Let us go forth therefore unto him without the camp, bearing his reproach. For here have we no continuing city, but we seek one to come.[2]

If those Christians who have gone on before us had sought to enhance their "positive images" rather than to bear Christ's reproach, the entire history of Christendom would have been altered.

2. The Law Demands Compliance

We now turn to a more substantive reason for compliance. The Minimum Standards, even though they are bureaucratic regulations, must be considered as "law." The statutory law in the Ohio Revised Code indicates that all schools in the State of Ohio are ordered to conform to the Minimum Standards. The OACS position reflects this argument repeatedly. The interview from *Ohio Schools,* mentioned above, goes on to say:

> Koloze explains that members of his organization believe that "God is the source of all power and government and that therefore we must be in subjection to the authority that is placed above us."[3]

This argument is further amplified in an OACS publication, the *Meaning of Membership* for the 1976-77 school year. It states:

> Much work has been done in accompanying Christian schools to the State Department of Education and working on their behalf toward maintaining a positive relationship as they become firmly established within existing laws.[4]

Let us note the language employed: "firmly established within existing laws" might be paraphrased, from the CSO point of view, "firmly ensnared within the unconstitutional bureaucratic controls." This opinion is written with absolutely no levity or sarcasm intended. It is deadly serious business. Before we comment further upon this position, let us consider one more statement made by Mr. Koloze on this subject. This quotation is from the Columbus *Citizen-Journal* of April 19, 1976:

> "There is no doubt our schools are all striving to achieve state charters, and we don't question the fact that we have to do it either," Koloze said.
>
> Koloze said about one-fourth or less of the OACS schools remain to be chartered.
>
> CSO does not want its member schools to be required to get a charter, [CSO President Dr. Roy] Thompson said.[5]

Having read these positional statements from the OACS, let us now summarize their argument. It might be put like this:

1. God ordains all power and government.
2. God commands Christians to be subject to the authority thus established.
3. The State Department of Education is part of our government and has established the present Minimum Standards.
4. Therefore, Christian schools are under a scriptural as well as a legal responsibility to comply with the Minimum Standards.
5. For this reason OACS does not question the fact that their schools must comply with the Minimum Standards.

This seems to be the reasoning that the OACS is following. It is possibly a more complete statement of their position than the OACS has made to date. CSO has, of course, considered this line of thinking. Let us now examine the weaknesses in this argument.

We know from Scripture that God does, indeed, establish the "powers that be (Romans 13:1)." We further recognize that God commands Christians to "submit [themselves] to every ordinance of man for the Lord's sake (I Peter 2:13, 14)." It is because of these and other Scripture verses that true, Bible-believing Christians are virtually always law-abiding citizens. Those who follow the Bible are not rebels, subversives, or insurrectionists.

But the Word of God lays down, in the same passages where Christian submission is commanded, certain limits upon governmental authority. In the Romans 13 passage we find these limits imposed at verse three:

> *For rulers are not a terror to good works, but to the evil.* Wilt thou then not be afraid of the power? *do that which is good, and thou shalt have praise of the same: For he is the minister of God to thee for good.* But if thou do that which is evil, be afraid; for he beareth not the sword in vain: *for*

> *he is the minister of God, a revenger to execute wrath upon him that doeth evil.* [emphasis added][6]

Civil rulers are the "ministers of God." They are responsible under God for rewarding those who do good works and for punishing those who are evildoers.

Again, in the I Peter 2 passage, the Lord places the same limitations upon rulers. We begin at verse thirteen:

> Submit yourselves to every ordinance of man for the Lord's sake: whether it be to the king, as supreme; Or unto governors, as unto them that are sent by him for the punishment of evildoers, and for the praise of them that do well.[7]

The same verses that tell us that God ordains rulers for service in government also prescribe how these rulers must discharge their ministries. Civil rulers are to reward good and punish evil.

Let us reflect momentarily upon this question. When the government uses its regulatory power to prosecute Christian parents for discharging their Biblical responsibilities by sending their children to Christian schools, has that government rewarded good and punished evil, or has it countermanded its responsibility before God? The answer, of course, is abundantly clear. As King David pointed out, "He that ruleth over men must be just, ruling in the fear of God" (II Samuel 23:3b). With this governmental limitation in mind, let us move along to the next consideration.

When the laws of men contradict the laws of God, the civil rulers responsible for passing the laws have clearly overstepped the limitations imposed upon them by Scripture. In such cases the Scriptures uniformly teach us to render obedience to the highest laws, the laws of God. Whether in the Old Testament or the New, God's people have always obeyed God rather than man — when there was a conflict. Examples of this truth are numerous. The "three Hebrew children" and Daniel are two prominent Old Testament examples. The apostles followed the same set of priorities in the New Testament. In chapter five of the book of Acts the authorities ordered Peter and the other apostles to cease teaching in the name of Jesus Christ. The well-known response is found in verse twenty-nine:

> Then Peter and the other apostles answered and said, We ought to obey God rather than men.[8]

Here was a case in which the rulers sought to overrule the commandments of God. The Christians were obliged to obey

God rather than men, for the law of God is the highest law to the Christian.

But, one may ask, do the Minimum Standards contradict the commandments of God? They do indeed, as we have seen repeatedly throughout this study. We may point to three major areas in which the Minimum Standards contradict the commandments of God:

1. They take from parents the primary responsibility to determine the education of their children. If the Minimum Standards are followed by all the schools in the state, then the only education available is statist education, for the Ohio Supreme Court has said that compliance with the Minimum Standards "eradicates the distinction between public and non-public education." For the state to assume primary responsibility for the education of children is unscriptural. See Deut. 6; Eph. 6:4; Psalm 78:1-8; I Tim. 5:8; Col. 2:8.

2. They take from the church the responsibility to control its own ministry of education, and they interfere thereby in matters of doctrine, matters of conscience, and the internal affairs of a church. This is unscriptural. See Acts 20:28; Eph. 4:11-15; I Peter 5:1, 2. This is also unconstitutional. Refer to Chapters 3 and 8 for detailed explanations of this fact.

3. They promote and require adherence to an antichristian philosophy/religion of education, which must be rejected by all Bible-believing Christians. This too is unscriptural. See Col. 2:8; Romans 12:2; and II Cor. 6:14-18. Refer to Chapters 4-7 for a detailed explanation of this fact.

The facts of these three contentions have been proven elsewhere in this study, and they have all been verified in the *Whisner* decision of the Ohio Supreme Court.

For these reasons we must disagree with Mr. Koloze's statement that "We don't question the fact that we have to do it [submit to state chartering] either."[9] We in CSO don't question the fact that we must *refuse* state chartering. Accepting a charter from the state violates God's commandments in order to submit to the commandments of men. "We ought to obey God rather than men."

Interestingly enough, Mr. Koloze seems to agree with us. Referring again to the interview in *Ohio Schools,* we find these paragraphs:

He [Koloze] said OACS believes that as long as govern-

> ment authority does not conflict with the instruction from the Bible, it is not objectionable.
>
> "If there has to be a choice though," he said, "we would choose the Bible way."[10]

Perhaps Mr. Koloze did not realize that the Minimum Standards do indeed "conflict with the instruction from the Bible." We hope that he, as well as other members of OACS, will re-evaluate the Minimum Standards in the light of the *Whisner* decision and in the light of the scriptural commands regarding parental responsibility, church polity, and doctrinal purity. If this is honestly done we sustain the hope that they may yet join us in our opposition to the state control of our Christian schools.

There is a second reason, legal rather than scriptural, why Christian schools must not comply with the Minimum Standards. There is a hierarchy of laws in our land. The Christian regards God's laws as primary, superseding all others, as we have seen. The highest law of the *land* is the Constitution, and it is followed by statutes, ordinances, and finally, regulations. Bureaucratic regulations, e.g. the Minimum Standards, are considered laws, but they are not equal to the U.S. Constitution. Sometimes bureaucracies promulgate regulations which are unconstitutional. When this occurs it is incumbent upon the citizens of this country to contest such regulations, for acquiescence to unconstitutional laws establishes them as valid. The U.S. Supreme Court has said (as we have already seen) that:

> The presumption of validity which applies to legislation generally is fortified by acquiescence continued through the years.[11]

Because the Constitution is the highest law of the land and does not violate our religious convictions, and because the Minimum Standards are bureaucratic regulations that violate both the Constitution and our religious convictions, Christians must not acquiesce to the Minimum Standards.

Furthermore, our attorneys tell us, an unconstitutional law is not considered as ever having been a law. It is void. **Pastor Whisner and his co-defendants, therefore, never broke the law.** They refused to comply with an unconstitutional set of regulations, and in doing so they upheld the U.S. Constitution. They did not meet the Minimum Standards, they were charged as criminals, but they were and are innocent of the charges. In order that the other Christian schools do not fortify the validity of the unconstitutional Minimum Standards, they must refuse, on the basis of religious conviction, to comply with these Standards.

In response to the OACS argument that the law demands compliance with the Minimum Standards by Christian schools, we answer that a higher law, the law of God, forbids compliance. We also answer that Christian schools must refuse to comply, in order that they might not validate an unconstitutional law to the detriment of the generations which follow ours.

3. The Minimum Standards and Educational Opportunities

One principal of an OACS school has stated the following, according to a newspaper interview:

> We would like to provide all the opportunities that our students need, academically, socially and spiritually. We're looking for a better product than what our friends, the public schools, can produce.[12]

This statement was made in defense of the use of the Minimum Standards by Christian schools. Because the Minimum Standards require the teaching of many subjects and require many student services, this principal apparently felt that compliance was necessary to provide excellence in educational opportunities.

Our answer to this contention is simple enough. Christian schools can, and should, and do *voluntarily* offer all the educational opportunities which they deem necessary, consistent with their religious convictions, and which they are able, without tax monies, to incorporate into their programs. Christian schools are interested primarily in training children in a Christian atmosphere and a Christian philosophy of education, in furnishing their students with sound academic preparation, and in preparing students for future obligations and responsibilities as adults. A Christian school does not need to be coerced into providing that which is contributory to a sound Christian education. Many of the items listed in the Minimum Standards, moreover, are frills where education is concerned. Our Christian schools are majoring in the majors, whereas the Minimum Standards spend a great deal of effort majoring in the minors.

4. The State is Responsible for Education

As this chapter was being prepared, a newsletter from one of the OACS member schools found its way to our office. This publication, *The Light,* is produced by the Worthington Christian Schools of Worthington, Ohio. *The Light* for December 6, 1976 has an article seeking to defend the school's endeavor to obtain a high school charter. The author of this article is not identified in the newsletter.

The Worthington Christian Schools have already received a charter from the State Department of Education to operate their elementary school, and the charter under discussion is for the high school. Most of the arguments adduced to defend the chartering of the Christian school follow the reasoning of argument number 2, given above. A new line of reasoning is introduced, however, that we have not encountered *from any Christian school heretofore*. For that reason we will carefully consider this article.

The writer argues that *the state is responsible for the education* of all *its* youth. Let us see how this conclusion is reached. The article begins by saying:

> Since the specific task of education was not delegated to the federal government nor prohibited to the individual states, Article X gives the states the authority, power, and responsibility for the education of their citizens. Thus Christians in the United States have the freedom to establish their own schools founded on a Christian philosophy of education which are under the general governmental oversight of the state in which the school operates.[13]

The writer for *The Light* has followed the thinking of the statist educators. In doing so he has ignored two very important considerations. First, the "authority, power, and responsibility" for the education of children does *not* reside in the state, but with the parents. The Word of God makes this abundantly clear in verses such as Psalm 78:5, 6 and Ephesians 6:4, and the courts of our land have consistently supported this parental right and responsibility. The following statement, only one of many which could be cited, is from the *Whisner* ruling:

> In three early cases . . . the [U.S. Supreme] court utilized the "liberty concept embodied within the due process clause of the Fourteenth Amendment to invalidate legislation that interfered with the right of a parent to direct the education, religious or secular, of his or her children. Thus, it has long been recognized that the right of a parent to guide the education, including the religious education, of his or her children is indeed a "fundamental right" guaranteed by the due process clause of the Fourteenth Amendment.[14]

The Ohio Supreme Court then goes on immediately to cite this language from the *Wisconsin* v. *Yoder* case:

> . . .The history and culture of Western civilization reflect a strong tradition of parental concern for the nurture and upbringing of their children. This primary role of the parents in the upbringing of their children is now established beyond debate as an enduring American tradition. . . .[15]

There is much more, but the above is sufficient to show that the *parents,* not the state, retain the primary role and responsibility in the upbringing and education of their children.

The "liberty concept" of the Fourteenth Amendment insures this fundamental right to all American citizens. The Tenth Amendment also supports this concept. The statist educators often seek to use the Tenth Amendment to give to the state the authority to control all education, and *The Light's* author has taken the same approach, as we have seen above. As we read the Tenth Amendment however, and apply it to the matter of education in general, and Christian education in particular, let us note carefully the last phrase of this amendment to the U.S. Constitution:

> The powers not delegated to the United States by the Constitution, nor prohibited by it to the States, are reserved to the States respectively, *or to the people.* [Emphasis added]

In the crucial area of educating children the courts have said that this is a power reserved "to the people." Christian parents and Christian educators ought to rejoice that this biblical principle has been upheld by the courts of our land. The writer for The *Light,* while trying to defend his own position, has fallen under the spell of statist educational thinking. In doing so he has surrendered a "fundamental right" which Christians, especially, must defend at all costs.

A second matter which was overlooked by the writer for the Worthington Christian Schools is that Christian schools are properly under the "oversight", not of the government, but of the church. We must never forget the religious nature of all education. All education is doctrinal and religious, and the education provided by a church school is therefore properly under the "oversight" of the church and the pastor. The Christian school is a ministry of the church, not of the state. I Peter 5:2 instructs elders to "feed the flock of God which is among you, taking the *oversight* thereof . . . ." [emphasis added]. See also Ephesians 4:11-16 and Acts 20:28-32. If Christian schools are to be governed by the state rather than by the churches, then we must immediately drop the name "Christian," for Christian they are not.

The writer for The *Light* next launches into a dissertation on Christian obedience to governmental authority. The thoughts in this section are the same as those in Mr. Koloze's thinking, presented above. Then the writer says:

> We are obligated by our Lord to be subject to those who are in authority over us unless it is clear that we are being commanded to live in disobedience to God's Word (see Acts 5:29).[16]

Parents in this state and others have been hauled into the courts, prosecuted as criminals and threatened with the loss of their children solely because they have exercised their God-given responsibility in the education of their children. How much clearer must it be that Christians today are "being commanded to live in disobedience to God's Word?"

To buttress his arguments on yielding to state control of his Christian school the writer next cites a passage from the philosophy of the state's Minimum Standards document! When one goes to the documents of the statist educators to support his point it is no wonder he comes to the same conclusions that they do. Not only does The *Light*'s writer cite the state's philosophy, he underlines it for emphasis. This is the portion cited:

> *Because of the importance of our educational system to the individual, the state, and the nation, the state must accept responsibility for insuring that all youth have an educational program in keeping with the needs of the individual and society.* [emphasis by The *Light*][17]

The state, according to their document and the concensus of The *Light,* has the responsibility for the education of "all youth." As we have seen in Chapter 8, that is exactly what the statist educators would like to achieve.

In closing the article, their writer has made this statement:

> It is our desire that God will *mightily* [emphasis theirs] use us for His glory in the preparation and education of the students He has entrusted to our care. Pray with us as we seek to utilize the *privileges granted us by our government* [emphasis ours] and in so doing honor the King of Kings.[18]

Once again The *Light* has taken the statist view of education. The responsibility to educate our young is a commandment from our God, not a boon from our government. It is a right reserved by the people, not a privilege "granted" by the state.

In arguing that the state bears the responsibility for the education of our children The *Light* has sided with the statist educators in opposition to the Word of God. This specious reasoning has been employed, moreover, in December of 1976, five months after the Ohio Supreme Court strongly upheld the responsibility of parents in the education of their young. Such reasoning is not only dangerous, it is inexcusable.

The *Light*'s article has been informative, in that it reveals the logical presuppositions that underlie the state chartering of church-operated schools. The deductive reasoning in this article may be summarized in syllogistic form:

Major premise: The state is responsible for the education of all its children.

Minor premise: Church schools are educating some of the state's children.

Conclusion: Therefore, church schools must be controlled by the state.

As we have seen above, the major premise in this syllogism is incorrect, both scripturally and legally, and that invalidates the conclusion.

Some Christian school educators in Ohio have recognized the error in the major premise above, but have nevertheless clung tenaciously to the conclusion. They have said, in effect, that the state must control church-schools, but that the state does not have the primary responsibility for the education of all children. This fuzzy thinking is inherent in the comments quoted in the previous arguments in favor of Christian school compliance with the Minimum Standards. CSO's position may be syllogistically represented as follows:

Major premise: The state must not interfere with religion.

Minor premise: Christian education is part of our religion.

Conclusion: Therefore the state must not interfere with Christian education.

This is, of course, a simplified expression of our contentions, but it was exactly this reasoning that was validated by the Ohio Supreme Court in the *Whisner* decision.

In summary of this argument, that the state is responsible for the education of all youth, we have seen that it is scripturally and legally erroneous. We have dealt with it at length because this is actually the underlying argument of all who defend the state licensure of Christian schools, even though not all of them have recognized it.

5. A Sham Education

This argument is included, not because it has been espoused in the written pronouncements of the OACS, but because it is a question that is raised when the "hands off" policy is discussed. The question is this: If the state does not control Christian schools, how can the children be protected from a sham education? Let us examine three responses to this question.

First, it is the responsibility of parents to determine the education of their children. The U.S. Supreme Court, the Ohio Supreme Court, and many other courts of our land have upheld this basic right. Despite the declamations of the "professional," elitist educators to the contrary, parents *are* competent to determine whether their children are being properly educated. It would appear that parents, in most cases, are more competent to judge in this matter than are the "experts."

Second, the payment of tuition in nonpublic schools is a prohibition against a sham education. Virtually all parents who spend additional money, above and beyond their tax payments, solely for the education of their children, are careful to be certain that they are receiving their money's worth. Few parents are willing to support a school, even a Christian school, that fails to deliver a superior academic product. A sham school will fold from lack of students.

Third, the academic progress in Christian schools generally has been excellent, whereas the academic progress of the public schools, which are all state chartered, has been under constant criticism for many years. State chartering obviously does not prevent the public schools from giving a sham education. The public educational systems in Ohio and elsewhere are drawing the criticism of "educational malpractice." It is an awful shame that altogether too many children in the public schools are being deprived of a decent education despite the lavish outpouring of money, talent, and energy into the schools. Consider, for example, these statistics for *public* schools:

> Some 35 percent of those who have completed five years of school will be functionally illiterate. Children will not be able to add, subtract, multiply, or divide. Scholastic Aptitude Tests will continue their drastic decline in scores. All the disastrous educational innovations of the 60s, found to be failures in the early 70s will still be very much in existence. Textbook publishers, responding to a changing market in college texts, will continue to use simplified language in their books because large numbers of college students simply cannot read the English language well enough to understand textbooks previously

used and understood by college students. One-third of our young men will flunk the Armed Forces Qualifying Examination, which means they can neither read, write, spell, or compute on a 5th grade level. National publications and weekly magazines will continue to print articles about the shocking state of education. Brig. Gen. William Woodyard, Dean of the faculty of the Air Force Academy, has stated that more than 300 freshmen cadets will have to take remedial courses in English and mathematics.

Many students who graduated from high school with top grades will find that they can't make it in college — even with their college textbooks now written at a 9th grade level. Many college graduates who received their diplomas this year will find out that they were not actually given the academic prerequisites necessary for a productive life in the working world, but simply received their diplomas based on inflated grades of A or B, due to the fact that their college didn't give anyone a grade lower than C, making it impossible for anyone to fail. James Kilpatrick, noted columnist put it quite bluntly: "We are raising a whole nation of 'culturally disadvantaged children' " and "education is a sordid, sorry racket."[19]

With an indictment such as this, it is clear that the State Departments of Education — in Ohio and the other states — have enough work to keep them busy just in trying to straighten out the tragic travesty known as "public education." Yet, the Christian schools are reporting superior academic results almost universally. The Christian schools do not need the guidance of an Orwellian Big Brother to protect children from a sham education. Rather, it is clear, the children in the various states need the guidance of concerned Christian people to protect them from the sometimes bumbling, sometimes intentional, havoc created by the "big brother" educators.

6. *College Acceptance of Students*

Another argument posited in favor of state licensure or state approval is the one suggesting that students graduated from Christian schools which are not approved by the State Department of Education will be unable to secure admission to the colleges of their choice. This is simply inaccurate.

Many colleges today are virtually begging for students because the number of potential students has declined significantly. College admissions are usually based on the achievement scores of the college entrance tests, rather than on the approval or non-approval of Christian elementary and secondary schools.

Most, if not all, Christian colleges and universities are said to follow this same policy.

The matter of college admissions is not a viable argument in favor of the chartering of Christian schools.

7. *Acceptance at Grade Level for Transfer Students*

We come now to a more substantive reason. If a student attends a non-chartered Christian school for one or more years, and must then transfer back into the public schools, for any reason (expulsion, financial problems, etc.), will the public schools recognize his work done in the non-chartered school and admit him at his proper grade level?

Thus far in Ohio, we know of no child who was refused admittance to a public school at his grade level due to attendance in a non-chartered Christian school. The question has come up, but our attorneys inform us that should a public school attempt this practice, serious constitutional questions would be brought into focus. If the situation warranted it, we would pursue the necessary litigation to see that a child was not deprived of his rights in this way. It would be preferable to fight, if necessary, than to surrender our convictions and our church-schools to the control of the educational bureaucracy. This is because our convictions are truly held.

In this matter, expediency might lead to acceptance of a state charter, but conviction militates against it. **Christians are not to base their decisions on what is easy, but upon what is right.** Based upon conviction then, we reject this final argument in favor of the chartering of Christian schools.

Reasons Against Compliance

Many Christian educators in Ohio and around the nation are thoughtfully considering or reconsidering the question of state licensure, or state chartering, of Christian schools subsequent to the landmark *Whisner* decision. In that decision, as we have seen, the Ohio Supreme Court declared that the Minimum Standards are unconstitutionally applied to a church-operated school which holds religious convictions against compliance.

This entire study has been written to present the reasons why CSO believes that Christian schools in Ohio must not comply with the Ohio Minimum Standards, and why Christian schools in general must avoid the state control, or state licensure, of their church-operated schools. The previous chapters explore these reasons in detail and provide documentation to support the CSO position. We will now survey these major arguments against compliance in summary form. Anyone seeking more information on these arguments should re-read the material indicated under each summary.

1. The "WHOLE THING" reason

According to the Minimum Standards a school cannot be chartered unless it surrenders to *all* of the Minimum Standards: "Chartering — requires compliance with all minimum standards."[20] The interpretative section also demands compliance for chartering:

> Level I details the academic and operational programs required for compliance with the minimum standards.[21]

What does the Ohio Supreme Court think about the "whole thing"? The Court says:

> . . .we must conclude that the compendium of "minimum standards" promulgated by the State Board of Education, taken as a whole, "unduly burdens the free exercise of [appellants'] religion."[22]

The Court further stated:

> In our view, these standards are so pervasive and all-encompassing that total compliance with each and every standard by a non-public school would effectively eradicate the distinction between public and non-public education, and thereby deprive these appellants of their traditional interest as parents to direct the upbringing and education of their children.[23]

For more information on this matter, see Chapter 3.

2. The PHILOSOPHY reason

During the *Whisner* trial an educational expert testified that the philosophy demanded in the Minimum Standards was that of Secular Humanism. The Ohio Supreme Court supported that identification.

Secular Humanism, as we have seen in Chapter 4, is a religion. The dictionary definition, the U.S. Supreme Court, and the Humanist Manifestoes all agree that Humanism is a religion. The religion of Secular Humanism, moreover, is the very antithesis of Biblical Christianity.

The internal evidence in the Minimum Standards' philosophy shows unequivocally that the Minimum Standards promote, teach, espouse, and require the antichristian religion of Secular Humanism.

The Ohio Supreme Court found that:

> The testimony of state witness John E. Brown disclosed that the interpretative comments [in which the state philosophy of education is given] form a part of the "minimum standards". . . .[24]

The Court also declared:

> In short, what the state gives to a non-public school through including a requirement in the "minimum standards" that the operation of the school must be consistent with its own stated philosophy. . .it takes away by compelling *adherence to all the "minimum standards," the effect of which is to obliterate the "philosophy" of the school and impose that of the state.* [emphasis added][25]

Secular Humanism is simply heresy to Bible-believing Christians, yet it is the philosophy of education presented in the Minimum Standards. Any school that complies with the present Minimum Standards thereby endorses, ratifies, and validates the philosophy of the Standards as to their school. What should Christians do? They should follow the instructions of the Word of God:

> For ye were sometimes darkness, but now are ye light in the Lord; walk as children of light
>
> Proving what is acceptable unto the Lord.
>
> And have no fellowship with the unfruitful works of darkness, but rather reprove them.[26]

And, furthermore:

> Now the Spirit speaketh expressly that, in the latter times, some shall depart from the faith, giving heed to seducing spirits, and doctrines of devils. . .
>
> If thou put the brethren in remembrance of these things, thou shalt be a good minister of Jesus Christ, nourished up in the words of faith and good doctrine, whereunto thou hast attained.[27]

For more information on this matter, see Chapters 4, 5, 6, and 7.

3. The REVOCATION Reason

Some schools have thought themselves "safe" from legal prosecution after receiving a charter from the state. The fallacy of this reasoning is given in the Ohio Revised Code, Section 3301.16. The law here says, in pertinent part, that the State Board of Education:

> shall classify and charter school districts and individual schools within each district. Such board shall revoke the charter of any school district or school which fails to meet the standards for elementary and high schools as prescribed by the board.[28]

In other words, what the Board gives, the Board can take away.

Officials of the State Board and State Department of Education have affirmed that there are *no* schools in Ohio, public or private, that meet all the minimum standards all the time. That means that a chartered school could be threatened with the revocation of its charter at any time. Some schools would surrender religious convictions in order to retain a charter. This has already occurred in the State of Ohio, according to what this writer was told by knowledgeable persons in one school.

And even if the leadership of a Christian school stood firm and refused to surrender more convictions in the future, what legal grounds would they have for such a refusal when they had already sought a state charter and raised no objections either against the Minimum Standards or against the state control of their school when they applied for their charter? Strict enforcement of the Standards and the revocation of charters could become a weapon of devastating effectiveness against Christian schools in Ohio which have sought or retained charters subsequent to the *Whisner* decision. Let us not forget how the Minimum Standards were used against Christian schools in the *Whisner* and *Canal Winchester* cases. When the State demands control over Christian schools, no one is "safe" by virtue of a charter.

For more information on this matter, see Chapters 3 and 8.

4. The GOOD FAITH Reason

Christians are instructed to refrain from both lying and deception. We must be men of our word. How can we then say, by word or deed, that we can comply with a document which espouses a philosophy of education contrary to Christianity?

How can we, furthermore, claim to believe the scriptural teaching that the parents are responsible for the education of children, if we surrender that responsibility to the state? How can we claim that our Christian schools are subject to the Lordship of Christ when we submit to the Lordship of Caesar? "No man can serve two masters."[29]

A Christian school purporting to follow both the Bible and the Minimum Standards is, whether knowingly or by delusion, involved in self-contradiction. This contradiction must be realized, acknowledged, and a choice must be made:

> How long halt ye between two opinions? If the LORD be God, follow him: but if Baal, then follow him.[30]

The issue we face is not new—it is merely couched in different circumstances than in previous generations. The issue is, Who is Lord? Is Caesar, or is Christ? We affirm that "Jesus Christ is Lord."[31] Let us then show that we are men of good faith, men who can be believed when we speak. Let us renounce the Lordship of Baal through the Minimum Standards, and let us render submission to the Lordship of Jesus Christ.

For more information on this matter, see especially Chapters 3, 6, and 8.

5. The RELIGIOUS LIBERTY Reason

The Ohio Supreme Court, in the *Whisner* decision, very clearly stated that the Ohio Minimum Standards violate the First and Fourteenth Amendments to the U.S. Constitution and Article I, Section 7 of the Ohio Constitution. These are the great religious liberty portions of the respective documents.

It is naive to suppose that the Minimum Standards violate the religious liberty of one Bible-believing Christian school, but that they do not violate the religious liberty of another Bible-believing Christian school with almost identical doctrine. Where is the rationale for such specious thinking? It comes from too much "public school expertise" being interjected into positions of leadership in the Christian schools and the Christian school movement. The issues we face regarding the control and oversight of the Christian schools are doctrinal; they demand the attention of Bible-believing pastors. It is the pastor who bears the responsibility before God for shepherding his congregation, and for leading them in sound doctrine:

> That we henceforth be no more children, tossed to and fro, and carried about with every wind of doctrine, by the sleight of men . . . whereby they lie in wait to deceive.

Too many pastors, it is feared, have turned over too much doctrinal responsibility and decision-making responsibility to those who are not, before God, responsible for such decisions. The oversight and control of the Christian school is properly reposed in the church, which is led by the pastor.

This does not assume that all pastors will lead their Christian schools in the proper way. Some are lacking in courage and others in the understanding of Scripture. But it is true that most Bible-believing pastors have a God-given jealousy for their people and their churches. A pastor who knows the teaching of Scripture on church polity, and who understands the religious and doctrinal nature of education, will take an unbending stand against state interference into the religious liberty of his church.

Public school educators, however, are used to taking orders from the state educationists, and they are used to thinking in terms of state approval. This is not to suggest, of course, that former public school educators who are born-again Christians may not effectively serve the Lord in Christian schools. Of course not. But it does underscore the necessity of scriptural training in the philosophy of Christian education. As we have seen throughout this study, the internal philosophy and operation of a Christian school is vastly different than that of the government schools. If our Christian schools have not withstood the Humanistic allurements in the matter of control, what level of Humanism is being taught in our classrooms as though it were "Christian" education? Unless we guard our Christian schools with jealous care, the Christian schools of our day will apostatize and destroy themselves just as the Christian schools of bygone days have done.

The beginning of that apostasy is the surrender of our religious liberty through the state licensure of Christian schools. In Ohio, some schools are well beyond the beginning.

For more information on this matter, see Chapters 3 and 8.

6. The PARENTAL RIGHT Reason

Both the U.S. Supreme Court and the Supreme Court of Ohio have said that parents, not the state, have the primary responsibility to determine the education of their children. In its *Whisner* opinion the Ohio Supreme Court cited this language from *Wisconsin* v. *Yoder:*

> . . .The history and culture of Western civilization reflect a strong tradition of parental concern for the nurture and upbringing of their children. This primary role of the parents in the upbringing of their children is now established beyond debate as an enduring American tradition. . . .[33]

The Ohio Supreme Court then went on to say:

> Under the facts of this case, the right of appellants to direct the upbringing and education of their children in a manner in which they deem advisable, indeed essential, and which we cannot say is harmful, has been denied by application of the state's "minimum standards" as to them.[34]

When a Christian school follows the route of compliance and

chartering, it forfeits thereby the opportunity for Christian parents who are serviced by that school to choose an alternative to state-approved education.

When a parent chooses a Christian school for his or her child or children, it is obviously because that parent desires something different than what is provided in the government schools. But the Ohio Supreme Court has said:

> In our view, these standards are so pervasive and all-encompassing that total compliance with each and every standard by a non-public school would effectively eradicate the distinction between public and non-public education, and thereby deprive these appellants of their traditional interest as parents to direct the upbringing and education of their children.[35]

This fundamental right — which is also a scriptural imperative — should not be casually cast aside as unimportant.

For more information on this matter, see Chapter 3 and the first portion of this Chapter. Compare Deuteronomy 6; Psalm 78; Colossians 2:8; Ephesians 6:4; and Proverbs 4:1, 10-13.

7. The CONTROL Reason

This argument against compliance is also called "separation of church and state." The Christian school is a ministry of the church, established for the same purposes and with the same mission as the church. It provides academic education, but academics are subsumed under the religious instruction. This is because education is a religious process; no education can be given in a philosophical or a religious vacuum. Education, therefore, is rightly understood as a process of religious indoctrination. As such it is properly under the control of the church rather than the state.

Control of the internal affairs of church-operated schools is equal to control of its supporting church. This control or oversight must be retained by the church if the free exercise of religion is to be protected. Harmonizing with both the constitutional doctrine of church-state separation and the scriptural doctrine of church polity, this position must be defended by Christian schools now, under the present Minimum Standards, and in the future when new standards are promulgated which would require the state control of the internal operations of church-operated schools.

For more information on this matter, see Chapters 3 and 8.

Summary and Conclusion

In the wake of the *Whisner* decision the question of the state chartering (or licensure) of Christian schools is a matter of primary importance. There are some arguments in favor of allowing such state control. Some of these arguments are weak, some are based on erroneous assumptions, and some are superficially convincing. All of these arguments, however, are set in proper perspective when the nature of education, the scriptural requirements of church polity, and the constitutional violations of the Free Exercise Clause are closely examined.

The arguments adduced in opposition to the state chartering of Christian schools show that this is not a question which allows an either/or response. State chartering of Christian schools is both wrong and foolish. It is wrong educationally, constitutionally, and scripturally. It is foolish because it surrenders to the government those powers of educational responsibility and control which rightly belong to parents and churches.

We will not halt between two opinions. State chartering of Christian schools must be refused.[36] We will pursue this stand calmly, dispassionately, and tirelessly, for our conclusion is based, not on preference, but on conviction.

[1]"Christian Schools: The Struggle Over State Regulations," *Ohio Schools,* February 13, 1976, p. 33.

[2]Hebrews 13:12-14.

[3]*Ohio Schools,* op. cit., p. 33.

[4]*Meaning of Membership*, the Ohio Association of Christian Schools, 1976-77, p. 12.

[5]Tony Mangine, Jr., "Fundamentalist Church Schools Thrive," *Columbus Citizen-Journal,* April 19, 1976, second section, p. 15.

[6]Romans 13:3, 4.

[7]I Peter 2:13, 14.

[8]Acts 5:29.

[9]Tony Mangine, op. cit., p. 15.

[10]*Ohio Schools,* op. cit., p. 33.

[11]*Life & Casualty Insurance Company of Tennessee* v. *Ossie McCray,* 291 U.S. 566 at 572, (1933).

[12]Art Toalston, *The Middletown Journal,* April 4, 1976, p. 25.

[13]*The Light,* (Worthington Christian Schools, Worthington, Ohio), December 6, 1976, no pagination.

[14]*Ohio* v. *Whisner,* 47 Ohio St. 2d 181 at 213, 214 (1976).

[15]Ibid., p. 214.

[16]*The Light,* op. cit., no pagination.

[17]Ibid.

[18]Ibid.

[19]Jo-Ann Abrigg, "In the Name of Education," *The Phyllis Schlafly Report*, December, 1976, p. 1.

[20]*Minimum Standards for Ohio Elementary Schools, Revised 1970*, op. cit., p. 3.

[21]Ibid., p. 19.

[22]*Ohio* v. *Whisner*, op. cit., p. 204.

[23]Ibid., pp. 211, 212.

[24]Ibid., p. 210.

[25]Ibid., pp. 215, 216.

[26]Ephesians 5:8, 10, 11.

[27]I Timothy 4:1, 6.

[28]Ohio Revised Code, Section 3301.16.

[29]Matthew 6:24.

[30]I Kings 18:21.

[31]Philippians 2:11.

[32]Ephesians 4:14.

[33]*Ohio* v. *Whisner*, op. cit., p. 214.

[34]Ibid., p. 216.

[35]Ibid., pp. 211, 212.

[36]This statement or any of the foregoing material is not to be construed as legal advice. It is presented as the convictional stand of Christian Schools of Ohio, and the Christian Schools of Ohio, Inc., recommends that an attorney be consulted before any person or Christian school takes any action with regard to the Ohio Minimum Standards.

10

God Help Us, Amen! Summary and Conclusions

We come now to the conclusions of our study of Ohio's Trojan Horse, the Ohio Minimum Standards. As we saw in Chapter 1, it was not the exterior of the Trojan Horse that destroyed Troy, it was the contents. We have examined the contents of the Ohio Minimum Standards, and we have found therein some very disturbing facts.

According to educational experts, Ohio's Trojan Horse is "educationally indefensible."

We saw that the objections to Ohio's Trojan Horse, however, are deeper than just the educational. There are also legal and religious objections. Legally, the Minimum Standards are unconstitutionally applied to a church-operated Christian school with truly-held convictions against these regulations. Religiously, the Standards are objectionable for several reasons. They interfere with the parental right to determine a child's education, they espouse a particular religion (Secular Humanism), and they require the state control of an integral ministry of the church, namely that of education.

The Ohio Supreme Court has judged Ohio's Trojan Horse to

be educationally, philosophically, and religiously "suffocating"; has said that total compliance with the Horse "eradicates the distinction between public and non-public education"; and has warned that adherence to the horse "obliterates" any philosophy held by the school only to "impose" the philosophy of the state.

We have also seen that the philosophy set forth in Ohio's Trojan Horse is one of Secular Humanism, which is both anti-christian and anti-scriptural. After reviewing the cardinal doctrines of the religion of Secular Humanism we have seen that the internal evidence of the Trojan Horse's philosophy proves the religious identification with Secular Humanism given by an expert witness and fortified by the Ohio Supreme Court.

"Quality education" and "the protection of the state" are commonly offered as the reasons why Christian schools must admit the Trojan Horse into their midst, but we have seen that the Horse's claim to these extravagant hopes is both deceptive and illusory. Attendant with the Horse, moreover, is the authority of the educational elite to control and oversee education to their appointed ends.

We have seen, finally, the reasons offered by some of the Christian schools which have already admitted Ohio's Trojan Horse. These arguments have been rebutted, and the arguments for refusing admittance to Ohio's Trojan Horse have been submitted.

Some of the conclusions of this study have been obvious during its progression, but we will now set forth the major conclusions in an orderly sequence. These conclusions do not, of course, purport to serve as legal advice, but are presented as a firmly-held convictional position. A Christian school planning to act on the matter of the Minimum Standards should seek competent legal advice.

First, the Secular Humanism of the public schools, and its decadent effect upon government education, should strengthen the resolve of *all* Bible-believing Christians that we must provide a scripturally and academically sound education for our young. Those churches already providing such an education are to be commended and encouraged; those churches not yet providing such an education are exhorted to begin.

Second, Bible-believing Christians in Ohio must recognize that the educational philosophy propounded in the Ohio Minimum Standards is manifestly one of Secular Humanism. Christians must insist that this philosophy be stricken from the Standards for it appears to be unconstitutional "on its face," as the attorneys would say. It is an establishment of religion, and it is therefore unconstitutionally applied to either the public or the nonpublic schools. Christians and other concerned citizens must *insist that the state not promulgate any philosophy of education*. The Department of Education is nowhere authorized to publish educational philosophy, and to do so is to automatically violate the First Amendment rights of those who disagree with any philosophy the educators may concoct.

Third, Christian schools in Ohio must be, and hereby are, warned of the dangers of compliance with the present Minimum Standards. Such compliance is legally suspect, scripturally unwarranted, and potentially disastrous.

Fourth, Christian schools everywhere must be, and hereby are, warned of the pitfalls inherent in *any* system of state licensure or chartering that interferes in the internal operation of church-schools. The Christian school is religious in every respect; it is a ministry of its sponsoring church. State control of a Christian school is state control of religion, and state control of religion is tyranny. Religious tyranny must be resisted if the freedom of religion is to be preserved for our posterity.

Elmer Towns prophesied the current conflict in his helpful work, and he explained it as follows:

> In the future, the new issue is the freedom of the Christian day school movement. The rapid growth of Christian schools is a threat to public schools. As the movement grows in quality and quantity, it indicts the public schools for their failure. Embarrassed public school educators cannot allow the Christian school movement to flourish. They instigate battles over *zoning ordinances;* local zoning boards say that Christian schools may not move into churches. The battle is enlarged by building inspectors, enforcing an unworkable code on Christian day schools. Still further, *the battle is carried on by state boards of education issuing varying objections from state to state, that no one can teach unless: (1) the school is accredited; (2) the teachers are licensed; (3) the number of hours of Bible classes per week is controlled; (4) curriculum offerings are regulated by the state board of education. All these matters are questions of freedom.* Can the Christian school teach what it feels is necessary for the pupil within its congregation? . . .
>
> *The public schools have not rested in their push for state control of education.* Public schools have filed lawsuits contending that they are responsible for education, while courts have historically maintained it is the parents' re-

> sponsibility. *There is coming a crisis of ownership: Who owns our children?* [Emphasis added][1]

The crisis of ownership is here; the battle for our schools, our children, and our faith is begun; the time to take our stand is now. The Word of God instructs us to "earnestly contend for the faith"[2] and the battle for our schools is the battle for our faith. The stand taken by CSO is a strong stand — a stand predicated upon conviction. In an age where the popular synonym for conviction is "bigotry" and the replacement for conviction is negotiation, such a stand will doubtless be criticized, its motives impugned, and its people maligned. But to stand upon conviction, to obey God's Word at any cost, is the requirement of those who love the Lord and desire to know His love (John 14:21, 23). Obedience to Scripture, not a "positive image" before the world, is the mark of a disciple. This obedience should be the goal of every Christian, and it *must* be the hallmark of Christian educators. If Christian educators, including pastors, refuse to stand on scriptural conviction, they will, by their example, train their students to approach convictional issues with a compromising attitude. We will train yet another generation of what Dr. Rushdoony calls "spiritual eunuchs" — weak men, incapable of acting ably for the Lord. By so doing we will have lost our "reason for being."

The delegates to the World Congress of Fundamentalists, held in Edinburgh, Scotland, in June of 1976, clearly recognized the need for a forceful and scriptural stand on the important issues of our day. These delegates "unanimously passed resolutions stressing obedience to the Scriptures."[3] The resolutions thus adopted reflect the convictional stand of Bible-believing Fundamentalists from around the world.

Two areas of resolution addressed by the Congress of Fundamentalists are critically important to this study.

First, let us consider the resolution "regarding the Church and the State."[4] This resolution read, in pertinent part, as follows:

> This World Congress of Fundamentalists believes
> 1. That religion and government can best work to achieve their purposes if each is separate from the other. *This wall of separation between the church and the state must be maintained impregnable.* [Emphasis added]
> 2. That personal rights of religious freedom should be guaranteed by every government to every individual.[5]

Once the wall of separation has been breached it is extremely difficult — perhaps impossible — to restore. Those Christians who willingly surrender their church-operated schools to the control of the government should be advised to thoughtfully consider the long-term results of their capitulation.

Second, let us consider the resolution "regarding the Family and Education."[6] The delegates unanimously affirmed as follows:

> This World Congress of Fundamentalists, believing that all men are possessed by God with certain inalienable rights in general and that those who are born-again believers have certain God-given privileges in particular,
> 1. Vigorously opposes all efforts by any government to usurp these parental rights of children;
> 2. Declares that parenthood is sacred, that God has made children subject to their parents (Ephesians 6:1), and that discipline is the parents' prerogative (Ephesians 6:4);
> 3. Recognizes that *God has raised up at all levels many Christian schools with unassailable standards to train Christian children in the essentials of learning and the skills of the spiritual warfare;*
> 4. Notes the increasing *pressure* that is coming upon the leaders *to surrender these freedoms* and God-given prerogative [*sic*], and *calls on all believers everywhere to vigorously oppose all legislation or pressures from government that consider it to be their right to limit or usurp the rights of parents by replacing the family with the state* and all the godlessness of anti-Christian control; *and to oppose such control even unto death in obedience to God's Word without regard to the consequences.* [Emphasis added][7]

These are strong words. To these resolutions as well as the others from the Congress we say a hearty, "Amen!" These are matters of scriptural conviction, and Christian people must live and die by conviction.

The battle for our schools, our children, and our faith has already spread to many other states as this study is concluded. The defendants in the several Ohio Christian school cases will be grateful if their experiences, their struggles, and their courage serve as a guidepost for their brethren who are to tread a similar path. And yet, for all the battles in Ohio, the war here has only begun.

It is incumbent upon the Christians of our day to identify the issues we mutually face; to apply the Scriptures that answer our needs today; to clarify our stand; and to earnestly contend for the Faith. Christians of all ages have had to take these steps, and we are no different.

We will be well tutored in our stand to remember the words of the courageous reformer, Dr. Martin Luther. He was summoned before the powerful Diet of Worms, he was confronted with the charges against him because of the stand he had taken, and he was ordered to recant. He answered calmly, firmly, assuredly, with the courage born of conviction in these words:

> I cannot submit my faith either to the pope or to the councils, because it is clear as the day that they have frequently erred and contradicted each other. Unless therefore I am convinced by the testimony of Scripture, or by the clearest reasoning — unless I am persuaded by means of the passages I have quoted — and unless they thus render my conscience bound by the Word of God, I cannot and I will not retract, for it is unsafe for a Christian to speak against his conscience .... Here I stand, I can do no other; May God help me! Amen![8]

As we take our stand for our schools, our children, and our faith we must apply the command of the apostle:

> Only let your conversation be as it becometh the gospel of Christ ... that ye stand fast in one spirit, with one mind striving together for the faith of the gospel;
>
> And in nothing terrified by your adversaries, which is to them an evident token of perdition, but to you of salvation, and that of God.
>
> For unto you it is given in the behalf of Christ, not only to believe on him, but also to suffer for his sake.[9]

May the Lord help us to "stand fast in one spirit, with one mind striving together for the faith of the gospel!"

We have now seen why CSO has said that the Ohio Minimum Standards, as applied to Christian schools, are "unliveable." They are set before our schools as the Trojan Horse was set before the gates of Troy. They tempt us with promises of quality and accreditation. But we, unlike the Trojans, have looked at the inside of this Trojan Horse, and we have seen the danger lurking within. It is foolish to take a Trojan Horse into your school *before* you look inside, but what shall we say of those who look inside, see the danger, and take the Horse in anyway?

[1]Elmer L. Towns, *Have the Public Schools "Had It"?* (Nashville, Tennessee: Thomas Nelson, Inc., 1974), p. 98.

[2]Jude 3.

[3]Elmer L. Rumminger, "World Congress of Fundamentalists," *Faith for the Family*, IV (September/October, 1976), 9.

[4]Ibid., p. 10.
[5]Ibid.
[6]Ibid., p. 9.
[7]Ibid.
[8]J. H. Merle D'Aubigné, *The Life and Times of Martin Luther*, trans. H. White (Chicago: Moody Press, n.d.), p. 433.
[9]Philippians 1:27-29.

Selected Bibliography

Single-Volume Works

Adams, Richard G. *Who Owns Your Child?* Denver: Accent Books, 1975.

Bean, Joseph P. *River of Pollution*. Fullerton, California: Educator Publications, n.d.

__________. *The Source of the River of Pollution*. Fullerton, California: Educator Publications, 1972.

Bereday, George Z. F., and Jaan Pennar (eds.). *The Politics of Soviet Education*. New York: Frederick A. Praeger, Publishers, 1960.

Berkhof, L. *Systematic Theology*. Grand Rapids, Michigan: Wm. B. Eerdmans Publishing Co., 1965.

Boyle, Donzella Cross. *American History Was My Undoing*. Fullerton, California: Education Information, Inc., 1961.

Brauner, Charles J., and Hobert W. Burns. *Problems in Education and Philosophy*. Englewood Cliffs, New Jersey: Prentice-Hall, Inc., 1965.

Carle, Erica. *The Hate Factory*. Milwaukee, Wisconsin: Erica Carle Foundation, 1974.

D'Arcy, Martin C. *Humanism and Christianity*. Cleveland, Ohio: The World Publishing Co., 1969.

D'Aubigné, J.H. Merle. *The Life and Times of Martin Luther*, trans. H. White. Chicago: Moody Press, n.d.

Dawson, Christopher. *The Crisis of Western Education*. New York: Sheed and Ward, Inc., 1961.

DeJong, Norman. *Education in the Truth*. Nutley, New Jersey: Presbyterian and Reformed Publishing Co., 1974.

Dewey, John. *Experience and Education*. New York: Collier Books, 1974.

__________. *John Dewey on Education: Selected Writings*, ed. Reginald D. Archambault. New York: Random House, 1964.

Dollar, George W. *A History of Fundamentalism in America*. Greenville, South Carolina: Bob Jones University Press, 1973.

Drake, Gordon V. *Blackboard Power*. Tulsa, Oklahoma: Christian Crusade Publications, 1968.

Gaebelein, Frank E. *The Pattern of God's Truth*. Chicago: Moody Press, 1973.

Gehlmann, John, and Mary Rives Bowman. *Adventures in American Literature*. New York: Harcourt, Brace & World, Inc., 1958.

Glasser, William. *Reality Therapy*. New York: Harper & Row Publishers, Inc., 1975.

__________. *Schools Without Failure*. New York: Harper & Row Publishers, Inc., 1969.

__________. *The Identity Society*. New York: Harper & Row Publishers, Inc., 1976.

Havighurst, Robert J., and Bernice L. Neugarten. *Society and Education*. Boston: Allyn and Bacon, Inc., 1975.

Hilts, Philip J. *Behavior Mod*. New York: Bantam Books, 1976.

Hyles, Jack. *Satan's Bid for Your Child*. Hammond, Indiana: Hyles-Anderson Publishers, 1973.

Kienel, Paul A. *America Needs Bible Centered Families and Schools*. La Habra, California: P. K. Books, 1976.

__________. *The Christian School: Why it is Right for Your Child*. Wheaton, Illinois: Victor Books, 1974.

Lamont, Corliss. *Humanism as a Philosophy*. New York: Philosophical Library, 1949.

Love, Robert. *How To Start Your Own School*. Ottawa, Illinois: Green Hill Publishers, 1973.

Moore, Opal. *Why Johnny Can't Learn*. Milford, Maryland: Mott Media, 1975.

Myers, John (ed.). *Voices from the Edge of Eternity.* Old Tappan, New Jersey: Spire Books, 1972.
Park, Joe (ed.) *Selected Readings in the Philosophy of Education.* New York: The Macmillan Co., 1963.
Postman, Neil, and Charles Weingartner. *Teaching as a Subversive Activity.* New York: Delacorte Press, 1971.
Rafferty, Max. *Classroom Countdown.* New York: Hawthorn Books, Inc., 1970.
__________. *Max Rafferty on Education.* New York: The Devin-Adair Co., 1968.
__________. *Suffer, Little Children.* New York: The Devin-Adair Co., 1962.
__________. *What They Are Doing to Your Children.* New York: The New American Library of World Literature, Inc., 1964.
Reich, Charles A. *The Greening of America.* New York: Bantam Books, 1971.
Reiser, Oliver Leslie. *Humanism and New World Ideals.* Yellow Springs, Ohio: Antioch Press, n.d.
Rickover, H.G. *Education and Freedom.* New York: E.P. Dutton & Co., Inc., 1959.
Root, E. Merrill. *Brain Washing in the High Schools.* Wheaton, Illinois: The Church League of America, 1965.
Rushdoony, Rousas J. *By What Standard?* Fairfax, Virginia: Thoburn Press, 1974.
__________. *Intellectual Schizophrenia.* Philadelphia: The Presbyterian and Reformed Publishing Co., 1974.
__________. *The Messianic Character of American Education.* Nutley, New Jersey: The Craig Press, 1972.
Schaeffer, Francis A. *Back to Freeedom and Dignity.* Downers Grove, Illinois: Inter-Varsity Press, 1972.
__________. *The Church at the End of the Twentieth Century.* Downers Grove, Illinois: Inter-Varsity Press, 1974.
Schilpp, Paul Arthur, (ed.). *The Philosophy of John Dewey.* New York: Library of Living Philosophers, Inc., 1951.
Shirer, William L. *The Rise and Fall of the Third Reich.* New York: Simon and Schuster, 1960.
Silberman, Charles E. *Crisis in the Classroom.* New York: Vintage Books, 1971.
Skinner, B.F. *About Behaviorism.* New York: Vintage Books, 1974.
__________. *Beyond Freedom and Dignity.* New York: Bantam/Vintage Book, 1975.
Smith, Elwyn A. *Religious Liberty in the United States.* Philadelphia: Fortress Press, 1972.

Steinbacher, John. *The Child Seducers.* [Fullerton, California]: Educator Publications, Inc., 1971.
Towns, Elmer L. *Have the Public Schools "Had It"?* New York: Thomas Nelson, Inc., 1974.
Tsanoff, Radoslav A. *The Great Philosophers.* New York: Harper & Row Publishers, 1964.
Van Til, Cornelius. *Essays on Christian Education.* Nutley, New Jersey: Presbyterian and Reformed Publishing Co., 1974.
Wallbank, T. Walter, Alastair M. Taylor, and Nels M. Bailkey. *Civilization Past and Present.* Glenview, Illinois: Scott, Foresman and Co., 1967.

Reference Works

Barnhart, C.L., et al. *American College Dictionary.* New York: Random House, 1964.
Berry, George Ricker. *The Interlinear Literal Translation of the Greek New Testament: With the Authorized Version.* Grand Rapids, Michigan: Zondervan Publishing Co., 1969.
Halpin, Patrick A. "Church and State," *Encyclopedia Americana,* 1954, VI, 655-657.
Harris, William H. and Juith S. Levey (eds.). *The New Columbia Encyclopedia.* New York and London: Columbia University Press, 1975.
Metzger, Bruce M. et. al. *The Greek New Testament.* London: United Bible Societies, 1966.
Onions, C. T. *The Shorter Oxford English Dictionary on Historical Principles.* Oxford: The Clarendon Press, 1934, II, 1828.

Classical Work

Homer. *The Iliad,* trans. W.H.D. Rouse. New York: Mentor Book, 1938.

Scriptural Citations

The Holy Bible. All scriptural citations in this work are from the Authorized Version of 1611.

Periodicals, including Newspapers and Newsletters

The Columbus Citizen-Journal, April 19, 1976.
The Light, Worthington Christian Schools, Worthington, Ohio, December 6, 1976.
McClellan, Grant S. *Current,* Number 156, November, 1973.

The Middletown [Ohio] *Journal*, April 4, 1976.
North, Gary. "Educational Vouchers: The Double Tax," *The Freeman*, XXV, May, 1976, 259-275.
Ohio Schools, The Ohio Education Association, Columbus, Ohio, February 13, 1976.
The Phyllis Schlafly Report, Alton, Illinois, December, 1976.
The [Cleveland] *Plain Dealer*, July 29, 1976.
__________. July 30, 1976.
__________. November 27, 1976.
Rumminger, Elmer L. "You Shall not do this to My Child," *Faith for the Family*, Greenville, South Carolina: Bob Jones University Press, January/February, 1975.
__________. "World Congress of Fundamentalists," *Faith for the Family*, Greenville, South Carolina: Bob Jones University Press, September/October, 1976.

Legal Sources

Abington School District v. *Schempp*, 374 U.S. 203 (1963).
Everson v. *Board of Education*, 330 U.S. 1 (1947).
Life & Casualty Insurance Co. of Tennessee v. *Ossie McCray*, 291 U.S. 566 (1933).
Ohio Revised Code.
Ohio v. *Whisner*, 47 Ohio St. 2d 181 (1976).
Brief for Defendants-Appellants.
Brief for Plantif-Appellee.
Brief on the Merits of the Ohio Superintendent of Public Instruction as Amicus Curiae.
Brief on the Merits of Certain Ohio Ministers as Amici Curiae.
Transcript of Testimony
Pierce v. *Society of Sisters*, 268 U.S. 510 (1925).
Reed v. *Van Horn*, 237 F. Supp. 48 (1965).
Torcaso v. *Watkins*, 367 U.S. 488 (1961).
U.S. Constitution.
U.S. v. *Seeger*, 380 U.S. 163 (1965).
Wisconsin v. *Yoder*, 406 U.S. 205 (1972).

Government Publications

Minimum Standards for Ohio Elementary Schools, Revised 1970. Columbus, Ohio: n.n., 1970.

Ohio Elementary School Standards (Minimum) 1957. Columbus, Ohio: F. J. Heer Printing Co., 1960.

Unpublished Work

Rushdoony, Rousas John. "The State as an Establishment of Religion." Paper read at the Notre Dame University Law School symposium, April, 1976, Notre Dame, Indiana.

Tape Recordings

Rushdoony, Rousas John. "Humanism Versus Christianity." Lecture at the Christian Schools of Ohio Convention, Mansfield Baptist Temple, Mansfield, Ohio, October 14, 1976. Tape available from Christian Schools of Ohio, 6929 W. 130th St. — Suite 600, Cleveland, Ohio 44130.

__________. "Religious Goals of Humanism." Lecture at the Christian Schools of Ohio Convention, Mansfield Baptist Temple, Mansfield, Ohio, October 15, 1976. Tape available from Christian Schools of Ohio, 6929 W. 130th St. — Suite 600, Cleveland, Ohio 44130.